Take up
DRESSMAKING

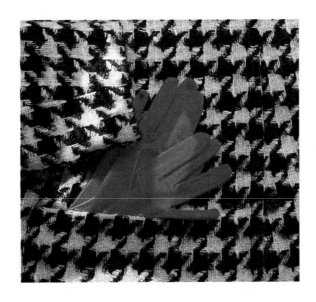

Take up
DRESSMAKING

SUE WHITING

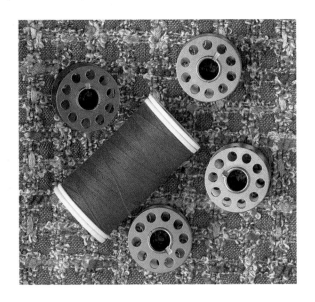

MEREHURST

This book is dedicated to my sister,
Caroline, who has always supported
and encouraged me in everything I do,
and to the memory of our mother,
Joan Ashman, who instilled in us both
a love of all crafts.

Published in 1994 by
Merehurst Limited
Ferry House, 51-57 Lacy Road,
Putney, London SW15 1PR

© Copyright 1994 Merehurst Limited

ISBN 1 85391 335 9

All rights reserved. No part of this
publication may be reproduced,
stored in a retrieval system, or
transmitted in any form or by any
means, electronic, mechanical,
photocopying, recording or otherwise
without the prior written permission
of the copyright owner.

A catalogue record of this book is
available from the British Library.

Edited by Alison Wormleighton
Designed by Kit Johnson
Photography by Di Lewis
Illustrations by Paul Bryant

Typesetting by
Litho Link Limited, Welshpool, Powys

Colour separation by
Fotographics Limited,
UK – Hong Kong

Printed in Italy by
New Interlitho SpA, Milan

CONTENTS

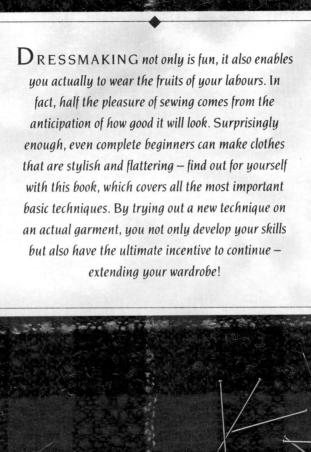

DRESSMAKING not only is fun, it also enables you actually to wear the fruits of your labours. In fact, half the pleasure of sewing comes from the anticipation of how good it will look. Surprisingly enough, even complete beginners can make clothes that are stylish and flattering — find out for yourself with this book, which covers all the most important basic techniques. By trying out a new technique on an actual garment, you not only develop your skills but also have the ultimate incentive to continue — extending your wardrobe!

Selecting a Pattern

*Before you can even start to sew, you
need a pattern. This will show you what shapes you need to cut
from the fabric and how to sew them together.*

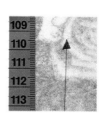

Choosing your size

Paper patterns, and also the diagram patterns in this book, are sized in the same way as ready-made clothes. All the designs in this book fit sizes 10, 12, 14 or 16 (equivalent in the United States to sizes 8, 10, 12 or 14), but purchased paper patterns often cover more sizes than this.

The three main measurements you need to take are your bust, waist and hip measurements. All these designs are suitable for a person about 1.64m (5ft 5½in) tall. Take your measurements wearing lightweight clothing – the measurements that relate to each size are actual body measurements and any additional room needed in a garment will have been carefully calculated by the pattern manufacturer.

Make a note of your measurements on the size chart below and compare them to the standard measurements for each pattern size shown on the chart. It is best to take them every few months.

Preparing your pattern

Once you have chosen the design you want to make and selected the correct size, you need to prepare the paper pattern pieces.

Many purchased paper patterns offer more than one style, or 'view', within a pattern. Sort out which actual pieces you will be using for the version you have chosen – there will normally be a list of which pieces are needed for each view – and separate these pieces from the rest. The smaller pieces are often printed together on one sheet and need to be cut out, leaving a narrow margin of paper around each.

If you are making a diagram pattern, like the patterns in this book, you will need to draw out your pattern pieces full size onto paper first. Follow the instructions given with each design which explain how to make your pattern. Large sheets of squared (graph) or plain pattern paper are available from good haberdashery shops (notions stores). If you

STANDARD BODY MEASUREMENTS FOR PATTERN SIZES

SIZE	10	12	14	16	YOUR MEASUREMENTS
BUST	81cm (32in)	86cm (34in)	91cm (36in)	96cm (38in)	
WAIST	61cm (24in)	66cm (26in)	71cm (28in)	76cm (30in)	
HIPS	86cm (34in)	91cm (36in)	96cm (38in)	101cm (40in)	

need plain paper, rolls of kitchen greaseproof paper (not available in the United States) are a much cheaper option.

Once you have all the pattern pieces you need, make sure they are smooth and flat before pinning them onto your fabric. If they are not, iron them with a cool dry iron.

Understanding your pattern

On each pattern piece there will be a series of different markings. Each of these markings tells you something you will need to know when sewing your fabric, and they should all be transferred onto the fabric pieces.

Cutting lines are the solid outer lines around each piece. On purchased paper patterns there is often a little scissors symbol somewhere along the line. This is the line along which you will cut out your fabric.

Seamlines are sometimes also shown on pattern pieces. A seamline is usually a fine line, sometimes with a sewing-machine foot symbol placed on the line. This line is the line along which you sew to join the pieces together.

Notches are the diamond-shaped marks placed along the cutting lines. They are used to help match up the correct points along a seam. A single notch along one edge will be matched to the corresponding single notch along the edge of the piece it is to be joined to, a double notch to a double one, etc.

Dots are used to mark the point at which you turn a seam, stop stitching or place a decorative detail.

Grain lines show you what direction to lay the pattern pieces on the fabric when cutting them out. It is very important to match up the grain line on your pattern to the grain of your fabric. If you do not, the garment will not hang correctly.

Place to fold lines are just as important as grain lines. On the pattern pieces where this occurs you will only have half of the finished section – you cut out the whole section by placing this line against the fold of your fabric before cutting.

Other details are shown in a variety of different ways. Take care to read the pattern to find out what each line or symbol means. It could be a fold line, pleat line, positioning line or buttonhole marking.

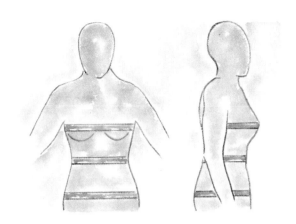

◆ Measure your bust around the fullest point, keeping the tape measure horizontal. Your natural waistline can be easily found by tying a length of elastic around your waist – where this settles naturally is your true waist. Your hips are about 20cm (8in) below your waist. Again, keep the tape measure horizontal and measure around the fullest part.

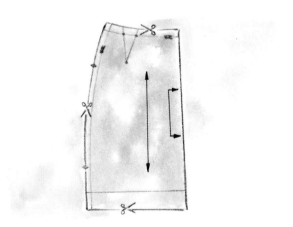

◆ This skirt pattern shows the cutting lines (solid outer lines with scissors symbol), seamlines (fine lines inside cutting lines, with sewing machine symbol), notches (diamond shapes), dots, grain line (vertical arrow) and fold line (on righthand edge).

CUTTING OUT

Once you have your paper pattern ready,
you can start to cut out the shapes that will make up
your garment – but you need to choose the correct type of fabric
to suit the garment you are making.

Selecting your fabric

Most fabrics fall into two major groups, woven and knitted. These two types refer to the way the fabric is constructed, not its fibre content or weight. Generally, **woven fabrics** do not stretch – they have a little 'give' across their width but no real stretch. On the other hand, **knitted, or jersey, fabrics** do stretch, and some will stretch in all directions, not just across their width. While it is possible to make a garment designed for woven fabrics in a knitted fabric, a pattern designed for use with a stretchy knitted fabric will simply not fit if you use a non-stretch woven fabric. Check your pattern to see what type of fabric you need.

The fibre content of your fabric is simply a matter of personal taste. Some people do not like **synthetic fibres**, but this does not mean they are not suitable for a design. However, a fabric with a high proportion of **natural fibres** will be much easier to work with. It can stand a hotter iron, thereby reducing the risk of damage, and in addition will be much easier to mould into the shape you require – a factor which is particularly important where there is a sleeve to insert into an armhole!

The other major feature of a fabric that will determine its suitability for a chosen style is its weight. In this book, fabrics are termed as light, medium or heavy weight. A **light-weight fabric** is the sort you would use for a blouse or petticoat, such as crêpe de Chine, fine cotton lawn or jersey, or voile. A **medium-weight fabric** is suitable for a dress or summer skirt, for example polyester/cotton poplin,

seersucker, linen, needlecord or printed cotton cambric. A **heavy-weight fabric** is the type used for jackets, winter skirts or coats, such as wool tweed, gaberdine, corduroy, velvet, brocade or coating. If you choose a fabric that is the wrong weight for the type of garment you are making, it will not hang correctly.

Understanding your fabric

Before you start to cut out and work with your fabric, there are a few points you need to understand.

It will usually be quite easy to work out which is the **right side** of your fabric. If you cannot tell the difference, then choose whichever side you want. Make sure you use the same side throughout the garment; some fabrics will appear different on each side in different light and at different angles.

Some fabrics have a design printed on them that looks different from one way than from the other. Other fabrics, like corduroy, have a surface finish, or nap, that lies in one direction. These fabrics are called **with nap fabrics** and it is important that all the sections are cut out in the same direction. Otherwise you could end up with flowers growing down the sleeves but up the body! Fabrics that look and feel completely identical from both directions are called **without nap fabrics**.

Cutting out the fabric

It is easiest to cut out fabric that is smooth, so start by pressing it. Choose a heat setting on the iron that suits the fibre content, and iron it smooth from the wrong side. If you are using a woollen fabric, steam pressing it now will pre-shrink it, so that your actual garment will not gradually get smaller later when you press each seam!

Most patterns give you details of how to fold your fabric before the pattern pieces are laid on it. This is usually with the right sides together and the two selvedges meeting at one side. Along the other side is a fold; this is the fold against which some pattern pieces may be placed.

Lay your pattern pieces on the fabric following the **layout diagram** which accompanies every pattern.

This will show you how each piece is positioned on the fabric. As you are usually cutting out through two layers of fabric, you only place each pattern piece on the folded fabric once, to cut a pair. However, you may need more than two of some pieces so remember to leave space to cut out these extra sections.

Once all the sections are pinned in place, check that none of the cutting lines are overlapping and that you have all the sections you need. Once you have done this, you can cut out your pattern pieces. Use long-bladed, sharp dressmaking scissors for this, and follow the cutting lines accurately.

LAYING OUT THE FABRIC

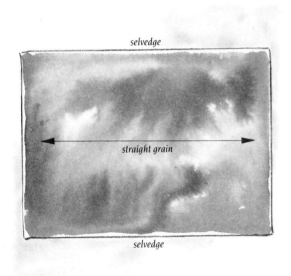

selvedge

straight grain

selvedge

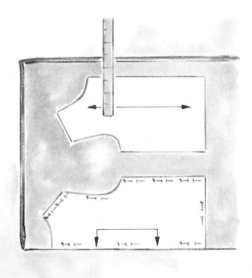

♦ The **selvedges** of your fabric are the two finished edges, which do not fray, running along the length of your fabric. The **grain** of your fabric is an imaginary line that runs along the fabric, parallel to the two selvedges. On your finished garment this grain line will usually run vertically along your body.

♦ Lay out your fabric on a smooth flat surface, folding it as specified in your pattern. Pin the pattern pieces to the fabric just inside the cutting line and make sure that the grain line on each piece follows the grain line of the fabric. Use a tape measure, or ruler, to check that both ends of the grain line are the same distance from the selvedges or fold. It is often best to start to pin each piece in place by pinning it to the fabric at both ends of the grain line.

Transferring the pattern markings

Once all the sections are cut out, you need to transfer all the paper pattern markings onto the fabric. Many people mark the **notches** by cutting around the little diamond shape along the cutting line, but this makes cutting out more difficult. A much easier way is to simply snip into the seam allowance at the notch point. Mark all **dots** using tailor tacks (see below).

NOTCHES AND TAILOR TACKS

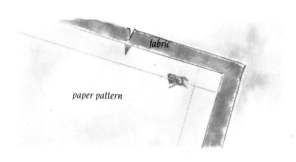

- Mark notches by simply snipping into the seam allowance for 4–5mm (³⁄₁₆in) at the notch point.

- To make a tailor tack, thread a needle with thread that will show up against the fabric and, using the thread double, take one small stitch through the paper pattern and both layers of fabric at the centre of the dot. Leave thread ends of about 8cm (3in) and then take another small stitch in the same place, leaving a loop about 15cm (6in) long. Cut off the thread, leaving ends of about 8cm (3in).

Once the dots have been marked, remove the pins and carefully tear off the paper pattern. Gently ease the two layers of fabric apart and snip through the threads between the two layers of fabric. All **lines** can be marked with lines of tailor tacks. Alternatively, lines and dots can be marked with a tracing wheel and dressmakers' carbon paper, following the instructions on the packet.

Interfacing

Once all the fabric sections are cut out, but before you sew them together, it is a good idea to cut out and attach the interfacing.

Interfacing is a second layer of 'fabric' that is attached to the main fabric in order to give it extra strength. This strength is needed in certain areas to stop the main fabric stretching out of shape (such as down the front of a jacket) or to stiffen the fabric so it will hold a particular shape (such as the collar of a shirt). Interfacing can be either a standard woven fabric, or a non-woven web of fibres.

A pattern will give you details of exactly which areas of the main fabric are to have interfacing applied to them. It can be the whole of a section (in the case of a collar) or just part of a section (in the case of a jacket front). The way the interfacing is applied depends on the type used, but it is always applied to the wrong side.

Sew-in interfacing is cut to fit the area it is to be applied to and basted in place just within the seam allowance. When the fabric sections are sewn together, the interfacing will be caught in the seams and the basting threads can be removed. **Iron-on interfacing** is much easier to use. It has a glue on one side, which is the side that is placed against the fabric. As it is pressed, the heat melts the glue, fusing the interfacing to the fabric section.

Interfacing is available in a variety of weights. Match the weight of the interfacing to the weight of the main fabric. If you are in any doubt as to which weight to use, choose the lighter option – once interfacing is applied it will appear heavier than it does on the roll. It is a good idea to buy a few metres (yards) of interfacing at a time, so that you always have some at hand when you need it.

BASIC STITCHING

*Once the fabric is cut out, you can start
to sew it together to make your garment. Apart from the pattern
and fabric, you will need a sewing machine and
a few other basic items.*

Equipment and materials

There are lots of different types of **sewing machine** on the market, and many of these will sew a wide variety of stitches. However, for most everyday dressmaking you do not need all these fancy stitches – a basic machine that will do a straight stitch and a zigzag stitch, forwards and in reverse, are all you really need. It is important to read through the manual that accompanies your machine so that you fully understand how it works. You will need **sewing thread** for the seams. A synthetic polyester/cotton thread is suitable for all types of fabric; it does not break easily, the colour does not run and it does not shrink when washed. Beware of cheap thread. Choose the colour to match

your fabric – if you cannot get an exact match, select a darker shade, rather than a lighter one, as this will be less noticeable on the finished garment. You will also need **basting thread**. Oddments of thread used for other projects are ideal for this.

Sewing needles will be needed, both for your machine and for hand sewing. Make sure you use the correct size and type of machine needle for the fabric you are sewing, as the wrong one will lead to uneven stitching. A size 9 (or 11) needle will be ideal for light-weight fabrics, a size 11 (or 14) for medium-weight fabric and a size 14 for heavy-weight fabric. A damaged machine needle will damage the fabric and, as it is often difficult to see that a needle is slightly bent, it is a good idea always to use a new needle when you start a project. Remember also to change the needle if you accidentally hit a pin.

For most dressmaking projects two pairs of **scissors** are adequate. You will need a long-bladed pair of shears for cutting out and a small pair of needlework scissors for snipping threads.

Pins are an essential part of any dressmaking box. Remember to discard any bent or damaged ones!

A **tape measure** or ruler will be needed when cutting out and, possibly, while making the garment.

Any other items of haberdashery (notions) that you need for an item will be specified with the pattern.

Basic seams

Most garments are made using a basic straight stitched seam. The pattern will tell you how much fabric should be taken into the seam – this is the seam allowance .

It's important to stitch straight lines for seams. Many sewing machines have a seam guide on the throat plate, which is a useful aid to keeping your stitching the correct distance in from the edges.

Adjust the length of the stitches to match the weight of your fabric. Most new machines give the stitch length in millimetres, while older ones give you the stitch length as being a set number of stitches per inch. For light-weight fabrics, use a stitch length of about 2mm (or 12–14 stitches per inch). Medium- and heavy-weight fabrics can be sewn with a stitch density of 2.5mm (or 10–12 stitches per inch).

Test out the stitching on a scrap of fabric before you start the actual seaming to check that the chosen stitch length does not cause the seam to pucker.

Once you are more used to dressmaking you will probably be able to simply pin the sections together before seaming them, thereby reducing the time taken on each seam by omitting the basting, or tacking, stage. But if you are a complete beginner, do baste the seams first. A little time spent here will be more than repaid by the time you save not unpicking wobbly seams and by the finished look of the garment. If you do decide not to baste, sew over the pins very slowly so as not to damage the machine needle – or remove each pin as you come to it.

Most seams are pressed open, but check your pattern, as some are pressed to one side. It is a good idea to have your iron and ironing board set up all the time while you are sewing. You will get a much better finish to your garment if you press each seam as it is sewn. One golden rule of all dressmaking is that you should never put a bare iron on the right side of your garment! If you need to press from the right side, cover the fabric first with a pressing cloth – an old clean tea towel is ideal. Match the heat setting of your iron to the fibre content of your fabric. As a general rule, the greater the synthetic content of a fabric, the cooler an iron it needs. Remember, too, that you should not use steam for synthetic fabrics – they may shrivel up or sag out of shape! Before you start, try out your iron on a scrap of the same fabric.

Neatening seams

Most fabrics fray (ravel) and, if the cut edges are not secured, or 'neatened', this can mean the seam may eventually fray so much that it falls apart! It is, therefore, very important to neaten the raw fabric edges. There are a variety of ways in which to neaten a seam, but the most effective and easiest way is to zigzag stitch over the raw edges once the seam has been sewn.

Use the same stitch length as for the actual seam. Match the width of the stitch to the weight of fabric or how easily it frays (ravels) – a narrow zigzag for a fine or firmly woven fabric, and a wider one for a heavy fabric or one that frays easily.

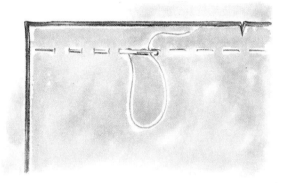

1 ◆ Start by pinning together the two edges that are to be joined. Place the pins at right angles to the edge and about 8cm (3in) apart. Take care to match any notches or dots along the edges.

2 ◆ Using one strand of basting thread, baste the two edges together. Use a **running stitch** as shown, making each stitch about 8mm (⁵⁄₁₆in) long. Place the stitches just inside the seamline, which will make it much easier to remove the threads later. Secure each end with a **backstitch** (one extra stitch worked exactly on top of the last one made). Now remove the pins.

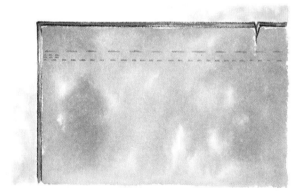

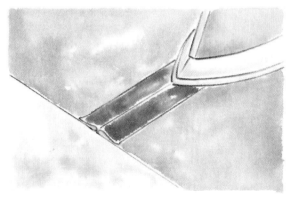

3 ◆ Sew the seam on your machine, stitching just next to the line of basting stitches, exactly on the seam-line. Take particular care to keep the line of stitching parallel to the fabric edges. To secure the threads at the beginning and end of the seam, sew a few stitches forwards, and then a few in reverse. Cut off the ends of the threads.

4 ◆ Press the seam open from the *wrong* side using the point of an iron, gently easing the two layers apart as you move along the seam.

ZIGZAG STITCHING RAW EDGES

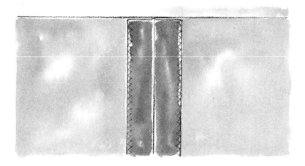

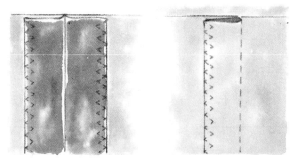

◆ After stitching the seam, but before pressing it, simply sew again along each raw edge using a machine zigzag stitch. If you can, try to have the righthand swing of the needle just over the raw edge, so that you completely enclose the cut edge in the stitching. Trim off any loose threads of fabric.

◆ Some machines have a two-step or three-step zigzag stitch, which is an even more secure way to neaten the edge. If the seam allowances of a lightweight fabric are both to be pressed to one side, the two raw edges can be neatened together.

MACHINE-STITCHING HEMS

1 ◆ A straight machine-stitched hem is a finish used on many casual garments as it is very secure and is quick and easy to work. Start by folding the required amount of hem allowance to the wrong side – your pattern will tell you how much this should be. Pin in place. Now fold under 6mm (¼in) along the raw edge, so the raw edge is hidden, and baste the hem in place 4mm (³⁄₁₆in) from this second folded edge.

2 ◆ Machine stitch the hem in place by sewing through all layers between the line of basting and the folded edge. If it is a circular hem, there is no need to secure the stitching at both ends with some reverse stitches; simply finish the stitching by overlapping the first stitches by about 1cm (³⁄₈in). Once the stitching is complete, remove the basting, and press from the wrong side.

SHAPING FABRIC

Few garments have all the shaping
they need in just the seams — there is often extra
fullness in a particular section. Style features such as pleats,
gathers or darts are used to reduce this fullness
and create the required shape.

Gathers

When an edge is longer than the one it is to
be sewn to, it must be gathered to fit, and
the extra fullness evenly distributed along
the edge in tiny folds. Sleeves, for example,
are frequently gathered into cuffs, skirts into waistbands, and the lower parts of blouses into yokes.

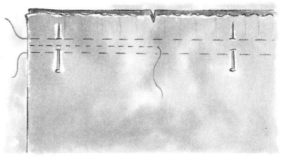

Sometimes a pattern will tell you to **ease in
any fullness**. Here you will find that one
edge is only a little longer than the other.
Ease in this fullness in exactly the same
way as you would gather an edge, but, as
there is less fabric, no tiny pleats will appear once the
edges are joined (if you have done it carefully!).

GATHERING AN EDGE

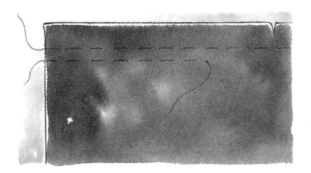

1 ◆ Start by working two rows of long running stitches
along each side of the actual seamline on the longer
edge. Use a stitch length of about 4mm (5–6 stitches
per inch) and sew with the right side of the fabric up.
Now pin the two edges together, matching any
notches and dots, and carefully pull on the two
bobbin threads (those visible on the wrong side) to
gently gather up the fabric.

2 ◆ Once the two edges are the same length, ease the
fabric carefully along the threads so that all the
gathers are evenly distributed. Complete the seam in
the usual way, securing the gathers as the seam is
stitched, forming lots of tiny pleats. As you stitch,
check that all the gathers are lying straight and
smooth. Once complete, remove the gathering threads
and any basting, and carefully press the seam.

Casings

Sometimes extra fullness is drawn in to form gathers by inserting elastic through a channel of fabric, known as a casing. This can be made using the actual garment section, or by applying another separate casing strip.

A **self-casing** is very similar to a machine-stitched hem – a 'hem' is turned to the wrong side to form a channel through which elastic is inserted. The width between the two rows of stitching that form the casing must be 3mm (⅛in) more than the width of the elastic you are using. If it is not, the elastic will not lie flat. Remember when you cut the length of elastic that the ends will be overlapped when they are joined, so you must cut your elastic slightly longer than you actually need it. The casing is then closed by either machining a row of stitches to complete the inner row of stitching, or hand stitching the seam.

With an **applied casing**, a separate piece of fabric is attached which will form the channel of the casing. This type of casing is usually used along a very curved edge or where there are pleats or other style details.

Darts

Sometimes darts are used to reduce fullness in one particular area. These need to be stitched accurately if the garment is to have the correct shape. Darts are usually pressed to one side. Horizontal darts are pressed downwards, while vertical darts are pressed towards the centre front or back. If the fabric is thick and would therefore be too bulky to press the dart to one side, carefully cut through the folded edge of the dart to within 1–2cm (⅜–¾in) of the point and then press it open.

Pleats and tucks

Tucks are essentially narrow pleats. Both are folds of fabric used to add extra movement within a garment without adding extra fullness. They can be partly stitched in place or left to hang free, and can be pressed to form sharp creases or left unpressed. If they are partly stitched, this stitched section is worked in the same way as a dart; the end point, however, does not fall on the fold but is positioned the width of the pleat/tuck in from it.

SELF-CASINGS

1 ◆ Fold the casing allowance to the wrong side, and then fold under the raw edge – as for a machined hem. Baste the casing in place close to *both* folded edges. Now machine stitch next to both folded edges. Form an opening by starting and stopping the inner row of stitching 3–4cm (1½in) apart, or, if the casing runs across a seam, carefully unpicking this seam between the two rows of stitching.

2 ◆ Using a safety pin attached to one end of the elastic, thread the elastic through the casing, making sure it does not twist as it is threaded through. Join the ends of the elastic securely and let this join now slide inside the casing. Close the casing opening.

APPLIED CASINGS

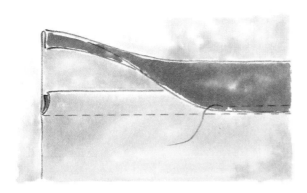

◆ Seam the casing strip in place and press both seam allowances towards the casing strip. Now fold the seam allowance to the wrong side along the remaining free edge of the casing strip. Fold the casing in half, bringing the folded outer edge of the casing strip over to meet the first stitching line, and baste in place. Complete in the same way as a self-casing.

STITCHING A DART

◆ Fold the fabric with right sides together so that the pairs of dots marking the dart match. Now baste the dart in place, placing the line of basting just beyond the actual stitching line. Stitch the dart starting at the widest end and tapering the stitching in to meet the fold at the pointed end. Fasten off securely at the pointed end by working a few reverse stitches.

PRESSED PLEATS

◆ For a pressed pleat, fold the fabric along the first fold line with the right sides together and baste along this fold. Now fold and baste along the other fold line, but this time with the wrong sides together. Lay the fabric flat, forming the pleat, and press the pleat. Remove the basting and press the pleat again to remove the indentations that may have been left by the basting threads.

LOOSE TUCKS OR PLEATS

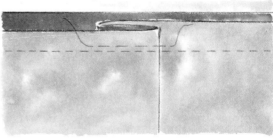

◆ For a loose tuck or pleat, fold the fabric along the edge to be seamed, forming the pleat or tuck, and pin it in place. Now baste the pleat or tuck in place, positioning the line of basting stitches just within the seam allowance. Once the seam is stitched, remove the basting.

SHORT AND SNAPPY

Take the short-cut to fashion with these stylish shorts.
With their simple, elasticated waist, which requires no zip or
waistband, they are simplicity itself to make.

YOU WILL NEED

1.05m (1¼yd) of 115cm (45in) wide fabric with or without nap

Waist length of 2cm (¾in) wide elastic

Matching thread

YOU COULD USE

Any light- to medium-weight fabric, such as the printed cotton used here, crêpe de Chine or viscose

SIZES

To fit size 10, 12, 14 or 16

Finished length from waist 42cm (16½in)

MAKING PATTERN

Following Pattern and Layout Diagram on page 67, draw out pattern pieces full size – one square represents 5cm (2in). Hem and casing allowances of 3cm (1¼in) and seam allowances of 1.5cm (⅝in) are included throughout. Transfer all pattern markings onto pattern pieces.

ADJUSTING THE SIZE

Pattern given is for size 12. To adjust size, cut through Front and Back pattern pieces along dotted line. For size 10, overlap pieces by 1.25cm (½in). For size 14, insert a strip of paper 1.25cm (½in) wide. For size 16, insert a strip of paper 2.5cm (1in) wide. Re-draw waist and hem cutting lines.

CUTTING OUT

Fold fabric in half lengthwise, with right sides facing, and pin pattern pieces to fabric following Pattern and Layout Diagram. Cut out all pieces and transfer pattern markings onto fabric.
From fabric: Front – cut 2; Back – cut 2.

MAKING UP

All seams are stitched with right sides facing then are pressed open unless stated otherwise.
1 ◆ Stitch Front to Back along outside and inside leg seams. Press.
2 ◆ Turn one leg right side out and slip this leg inside the other so that right sides are facing. Matching waist edges and inside leg seams, stitch legs together along centre front and back crotch

seams. Press the seam towards the left leg.
3 ◆ Fold 3cm (1¼in) casing allowance to wrong side around waist edge and turn under raw edge. Stitch casing in place close to both folded edges, leaving an opening in lower row of stitching to insert elastic. Press.
4 ◆ Cut length of elastic to fit waist, and thread it through casing. Join ends securely and stitch casing opening closed.
5 ◆ Fold 3cm (1¼in) hem allowance to wrong side around lower edges of legs and turn under raw edge. Stitch hem in place close to inner edge. Press.

SOFT OPTIONS

*You've no less than four options with this skirt, all
of them quick and easy to make: soft gathers or unpressed
pleats, and either knee-skimming or ankle-length.*

YOU WILL NEED

Pleated skirts

115cm (45in) wide fabric with
or without nap

Long skirt: 2.70m (3yd)

Short skirt: 1.80m (2yd)

Gathered skirts

115cm (45in) wide fabric with
or without nap

Long skirt: 1.90m (2⅛yd)

Short skirt: 1.30m (1½yd)

All skirts

3 waist lengths of 6mm (¼in)
wide elastic

Matching thread

YOU COULD USE

Any light- to medium-weight
fabric, such as the crêpe de
Chine used here, printed
cotton or cotton jersey

SIZES

To fit size 10–12 or 14–16

Long skirts: finished length
from waist 80cm (31½in)

Short skirts: finished length
from waist 50cm (19¾in)

CUTTING OUT

With fabric flat, cut the following:

Long pleated skirt

Skirt – cut three 84cm (33in) long
× 105cm (41½in) wide for size
10–12 or 111cm (43¾in) wide for
size 14–16; Waistband – cut one
12cm (4¾in) deep × 105cm
(41½in) wide for size 10–12 or
111cm (43¾in) wide for size
14–16.

Short pleated skirt

Skirt – cut three 54cm (21¼in)
long × 105cm (41½in) wide for
size 10–12 or 111cm (43¾in) wide
for size 14–16; Waistband – cut
one 12cm (4¾in) deep × 105cm
(41½in) wide for size 10–12 or
111cm (43¾in) wide for size
14–16.

Long gathered skirt

Skirt – cut two 84cm (33in) long
× 105cm (41½in) wide for size
10–12 or 111cm (43¾in) wide for
size 14–16; Waistband – cut one
12cm (4¾in) deep by 105cm
(41½in) wide for size 10–12 or
111cm (43¾in) wide for size
14–16.

Short gathered skirt

Skirt – cut two 54cm (21¼in) long
× 105cm (41½in) wide for size

10–12 or 111cm (43¾in) wide for
size 14–16; Waistband – cut one
12cm (4¾in) deep × 105cm
(41½in) wide for size 10–12 or
111cm (43¾in) wide for size
14–16.

Hem allowance of 2.5cm (1in) and
seam allowances of 1.5cm (⅝in)
are included throughout.

MAKING UP

All seams are stitched with right
sides facing then are neatened
and pressed open unless stated
otherwise.

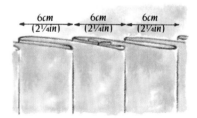

◆ *Pleating guide*

Pleated skirts

1 ◆ Join Skirt pieces together
along shorter edges to form a
tube. Press seams.

2 ◆ Fold 2.5cm (1in) hem allowance to wrong side around lower
edge of tube and turn under raw
edge. Stitch hem in place. Press.

6 ♦ Fold and press seam allowance to wrong side around remaining raw edge of waistband. Fold waistband in half to inside, matching pressed edge to previous row of stitching, and baste in place. Press waistband.

7 ♦ Topstitch (see page 27) around waistband 4 times through all layers close to upper and lower edges, and again 1.5cm (⅝in) from upper and lower edges. Press.

8 ♦ Carefully snip opening in waistband seam stitching between rows of topstitching to make openings through which elastic can be inserted. Cut 3 lengths of elastic to fit waist; thread each length through one of the 3 waistband casings. Secure ends of elastic and hand stitch casing openings closed.

Gathered skirts

1 ♦ Make as for Pleated Skirts, steps 1–3.

2 ♦ Skirt section has 2 seams that form the side seams. Run gathering threads along entire upper edge of skirt section.

3 ♦ Waistband seam is to be placed at one side seam – mark other side seam point along one long edge of loop. Matching one side seam to waistband seam and other side seam to marked point on waistband, pin waistband to upper edge of skirt. Pull up gathering threads to fit and distribute gathers evenly. Stitch seam, remove gathering threads and press seam towards waistband.

4 ♦ Make as for Pleated Skirts, steps 6–8.

3 ♦ Join ends of Waistband to form a circle. Press seam.

4 ♦ Skirt section has 3 seams. One goes at centre back, and other 2 fall just forward of where side seams would normally be. Following diagram on page 22 and starting at centre back seam, fold, pin and baste 6cm (2¼in) deep pleats all around upper edge. For size 10–12 make 17 pleats, and for size 14–16 make 18 pleats.

5 ♦ Matching centre back seams of skirt to waistband seam, sew waistband to upper edge of skirt. Press seam towards waistband.

FINISHING EDGES

*Not all the outer
edges of a garment are always finished
with a simple machine-stitched hem – sometimes the hem
is stitched by hand, or a facing, binding
or band is applied.*

Facings

Sometimes a shaped edge is finished with a facing. This is a piece of fabric that is attached to the edge and then folded to the wrong side. It is usually totally invisible from the right side and will frequently have seams that echo the seams of the outer section. Facings are usually interfaced and, to avoid bulk, the inner edge of these should be neatened with a row of stitching, rather than with a machined hem.

Bands

When only part of the facing is folded to the wrong side, leaving a section to show from the right side, the facing will form a band of fabric along the finished edge. Make and attach this band to the main section in exactly the same way as an applied casing (see pages 18–19). But remember to look at your pattern to see where the stitching is placed. Frequently the inner folded edge of a band will be hand stitched in place so that no stitching is visible from the right side. Hand-stitch the edge in position as shown on page 26, using one strand of thread and taking each stitch through the folded edge and main section along the seamline – one hand stitch for every 3–4 machine stitches should be sufficient.

Bias binding

Purchased bias binding, a narrow strip of fabric cut diagonally across the grain, is a good way to finish curved edges. Available in many colours and widths, it has folds pressed into it – these form the seamlines. It can be attached so that half of the binding is visible from the right side or so that it is completely invisible from the right side; both methods are shown on page 26. You can also make your own bias binding (see pages 52–3 for how to do this).

Hand-stitched hems

For this type of hem, sometimes known as blind hemming stitch, the stitching should be virtually invisible from both the right side and the wrong side. As the inner raw edge is not turned under, there is less bulk, making it ideal for heavy or bulky fabrics.

Before you start, neaten and press the raw edge, then fold and baste the hem allowance in place, positioning the line of basting stitches 1cm (⅜in) below the neatened edge. Thread a needle with matching thread and fold the main garment sections down away from the neatened edge. Work blind hemming stitch as shown on page 27, taking tiny horizontal stitches through just one or two threads.

Once the stitching is complete, remove the basting thread and press the hem. Press the folded hem edge first, keeping the iron away from the neatened edge, and then carefully press the upper edge, sliding the nose of the iron under the neatened edge. If you press over the neatened edge, you may leave the impression of this stitching on the right side.

♦ Start by making the various seams of the main outer sections and facing to the point where the facing is to be attached. Pin and baste the facing to the garment and make the joining seam in the usual way. If the facing goes around a corner, stop stitching at this corner point, with the needle in the fabric, then raise the machine foot and turn the work so that you are ready to sew along the next part of the edge. Lower the foot and complete the seam.

♦ To reduce the bulk of the entire seamed facing edge, the seam allowances should be layered. Trim away 6mm (¼in) from the facing seam allowance once the seam has been stitched.

♦ If a facing goes along a curved edge the seam allowance will need to be clipped to allow it to overlap or open out to fit the edge once the facing is turned to the wrong side. Cut very carefully into the seam allowance, stopping just short of the stitching line, at intervals of 1–1.5cm (⅜–⅝in). If stitching around a corner, the extra fabric at this point will need to be removed to reduce the bulk of the corner when the facing is folded back. Cut diagonally across the corner, taking care not to cut the stitching.

♦ Some garments have self-facings, in which the facing is cut in one with the main section. Part of the finished edge will be created by the fold line indicated on the pattern and the remaining section will be seamed in place. This is frequently the case with facings down the front of a blouse and across the top of a patch pocket.

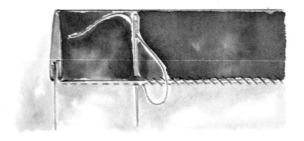

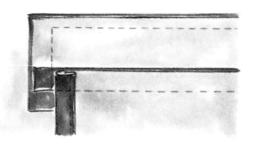

◆ For a facing that forms a band along a finished edge, hand sew the edge of the band in place so that the stitching doesn't shown from the right side. Working from left to right and using one strand of thread, insert the needle at right angles to the edge, as shown, taking a few threads of the band and one or two of the garment. Insert the needle to the left of the first stitch, again holding it at right angles to the edge. Continue in this way, making small, even, slanted stitches. Fasten off.

◆ Bands can be made in two pieces, one piece forming the outer section that shows from the right side and the second section forming what can be termed a band facing. Here, attach the outer section first and then the remaining section as though it were a real facing.

ATTACHING BIAS BINDING

◆ If the bias binding is to be totally hidden, start by seaming it in place with the right sides together, matching one fold of the bias binding to the garment seamline. Trim the main section seam allowance to narrower than the binding width and clip into the seam allowance as necessary. Now fold the binding to the wrong side and stitch the remaining free folded edge in place, either by hand or with a line of machine stitching next to the folded edge.

◆ If the binding is to be visible and will totally enclose the raw edge, start by trimming away part of the seam allowance along the edge of the main section. With right sides together and raw edges even, stitch the binding in place along one of the fold lines. Fold the binding over to the wrong side, enclosing the raw edges, so that the other fold line of the binding matches the stitching line on the inside. Hand stitch this edge in place. Press.

BLIND HEMMING STITCH

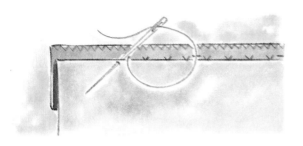

♦ Using one thickness of thread, secure the thread to the edge of the hem allowance. Working from right to left, take a stitch through the hem allowance and then pick up one or two threads from the folded edge of the garment. Continue along the hem edge in this way, making each stitch through the folded edge 8–12mm (⅜–½in) apart and working a backstitch (see page 15) through the hem allowance every 8–10cm (3–4in) to secure the thread.

TOPSTITCHING

♦ Whether a finished edge has binding, a facing or a band attached to it, it may also have a decorative line of topstitching. Wherever possible, work this line of topstitching with the right side up. Use the machine foot or the throat-plate guide to help you keep the stitching an even distance in from the finished edge.

EASY ELEGANCE

To achieve the clean lines of this elegant cardigan-style jacket, the edges are finished with neat facings. Patch pockets add just the right amount of detail.

YOU WILL NEED

1.70m (1⅞yd) of 150cm (60in) wide fabric with or without nap

90cm (1yd) of 90cm (36in) wide iron-on interfacing

3 stud fasteners (snaps)

Matching thread

YOU COULD USE

Any medium-weight fabric, such as the cotton cambric used here, needlecord or printed viscose

SIZES

To fit size 10, 12–14, or 16

Finished length from back neck 72cm (28¼in)

MAKING PATTERN

Following Pattern and Layout Diagram on page 67, draw out pattern pieces full size – one square represents 5cm (2in). Hem allowance of 4cm (1½in) and seam allowances of 1.5cm (⅝in) are included throughout. Transfer all pattern markings onto pattern pieces.

ADJUSTING THE SIZE

Pattern given is for size 12–14. To adjust size, cut through Front and Back pattern pieces along dotted line. For size 10, overlap pieces by 1.5cm (⅝in). For size 16, insert a strip of paper 1.5cm (⅝in) wide. Re-draw shoulder and hem cutting lines.

CUTTING OUT

Fold fabric in half lengthwise, with right sides facing, and pin pattern pieces to fabric following Pattern and Layout Diagram. Cut out all pieces and transfer markings.

From fabric: Front – cut 2; Back – cut one to fold; Pocket – cut 2; Front Facing – cut 2; Back Neck Facing – cut one to fold; Sleeve – cut 2; Cuff Facing – cut 2.

From interfacing: Front Facing – cut 2; Back Neck Facing – cut one to fold.

MAKING UP

All seams are stitched with right sides facing then are pressed open unless stated otherwise.

1 ♦ Fold 4cm (1½in) self-facing to right side across top of each Pocket and fold 6mm (¼in) back towards wrong side across raw edge. Stitch across ends. Trim seam

and turn facing to wrong side. Press, pressing seam allowance to wrong side along remaining edges. Topstitch across Pocket close to folded edge of self-facing. Press.

2 ♦ Place Pockets onto Fronts, 8cm (3in) above lower edge of Front and 12cm (4¾in) in from front opening edge. Topstitch close to side and lower edges. Press.

3 ♦ Stitch Fronts to Back along shoulder and side seams. Press.

4 ♦ Apply interfacing to wrong side of Front Facings and Back Neck Facing. Stitch facing shoulder seams and press. Neaten inner edge.

5 ♦ Matching shoulder seams and notches, stitch facings to front opening and neck edges of body section, stitching across lower edge of Front Facings 4cm (1½in) above raw edge. Trim seam and corners, clip curves and turn facing to inside. Press.

6 ♦ Fold 4cm (1½in) hem allowance to wrong side along remaining lower edge of body section. Turn under raw edge and baste hem in place, continuing basting along inner edge of facings. Topstitch hem, front opening and neck edges close to finished edge and again 3cm (1¼in) away. Press.

7 ◆ Stitch Sleeve seams and press – note that seam is *not* at under-arm, but positioned towards back of Sleeve.

8 ◆ Stitch ends of Cuff Facings together to form loops; press. Neaten upper, unnotched edge of Cuff Facings.

9 ◆ Matching seams and notches, stitch Cuff Facing to lower edge of Sleeve. Trim and clip seam. Turn to wrong side. Press, placing seam along edge. Topstitch close to and 3cm (1¼in) from edge.

10 ◆ Matching notches and sleeve dots to side and shoulder seams, stitch Sleeves into armholes. Press seam towards Sleeve.

11 ◆ Following instructions on packet, attach stud fasteners to Fronts. Position top stud 1cm (⅜in) below neck slope corner along front opening edge, and remaining studs 13cm (5in) apart.

FIT TO BE TIED

*You can create any number of looks from
this versatile kimono pattern, simply by varying the fabric.
If desired, the patch pockets, tie belt and front
band can be in a contrasting fabric.*

YOU WILL NEED

2.90m (3¼yd) of 150cm
(60in) wide fabric with or
without nap

Matching thread

YOU COULD USE

Any light- to medium-
weight fabric, such as the
crêpe de Chine used here,
cotton, seersucker, a light-
weight woollen cambric or
towelling (terrycloth)

SIZES

To fit size 10, 12–14 or 16

Finished length from back
neck 108cm (42½in)

MAKING PATTERN

Following Pattern and Layout Diagram on page 69, draw out pattern
pieces full size – one square
represents 5cm (2in). Hem allowance of 3cm (1¼in) and seam
allowances of 1.5cm (⅝in) are
included throughout the pattern
pieces. Transfer all pattern markings onto pattern pieces.

ADJUSTING THE SIZE

Pattern given is **for size 12–14**. To
adjust size, cut through Front and
Back pattern pieces along dotted
line. **For size 10**, overlap pieces by
1.5cm (⅝in). **For size 16**, insert a
strip of paper 1.5cm (⅝in) wide.
Re-draw the shoulder and hem
cutting lines.

CUTTING OUT

Fold fabric in half lengthwise, with
right sides facing, and pin pattern
pieces to fabric following Pattern
and Layout Diagram. Cut out all
pieces and transfer pattern markings onto fabric.

From fabric: Front – cut 2; Back –
cut one to fold; Pocket – cut 2;
Front Band – cut 2; Sleeve – cut 2;
Belt – cut 2; Belt Loops – cut 2.

MAKING UP

All seams are stitched with right
sides facing then are pressed
open unless stated otherwise.

1 ◆ Neaten all edges of Pockets.
Fold 6cm (2¼in) self-facing to
right side across top of each
Pocket and stitch across ends of
facing. Trim seam and turn facing
to wrong side. Press, pressing
seam allowance to wrong side

along remaining three edges. Topstitch close to and 5cm (2in) from
opening edge of Pocket.

2 ◆ Place Pockets onto Fronts,
positioning Pockets 12cm (4¾in)
in from front opening edge and
33cm (13in) above lower edge.
Topstitch in place close to side
and lower edges. Press.

3 ◆ Stitch Fronts to Back across
shoulder seams. Press.

4 ◆ Matching Sleeve dot to shoulder seam, stitch Sleeves to body
sections along armhole edge.
Press seam towards Sleeve.

5 ◆ Matching armhole seams,
stitch sleeve and side seams in
one operation. Press.

6 ◆ Fold the 3cm (1¼in) hem
allowance to wrong side along
lower edge of body sections and
turn under raw edge. Topstitch in
place close to second folded
edge. Press.

7 ◆ Join notched ends of Bands to
form one long strip. Press. Press
seam allowance to wrong side
along one long edge.

8 ◆ Positioning ends of Bands
1.5cm (⅝in) beyond hem edge of
body sections, matching notches,
dots to shoulder seams and centre back points, stitch remaining

long edge of Bands to front opening and neck edges of body sections. Press seam towards Band.

9 ◆ Fold Band in half with right sides together and stitch across ends. Turn Band right side out and press ends. Bring pressed edge of Band over to match stitching line on inside and neatly slip-stitch in place. Press. Topstitch Band close to inner seam line. Press.

10 ◆ Fold 3cm (1¼in) hem allowance to wrong side along lower edge of Sleeves and turn under raw edge. Topstitch in place close to second folded edge. Press.

11 ◆ Join notched ends of Belt to form one long strip. Press. Fold Belt in half lengthwise with right sides together and stitch along length and across ends, leaving an opening to turn Belt through. Trim seam and corners and turn Belt through to right side. Slip-stitch opening in seam closed. Press, placing seams along pressed edges. Topstitch close to all edges of Belt.

12 ◆ Fold each Belt Loop strip in half lengthwise with right sides together and stitch along length. Trim seam and turn strip right side out. Press, placing seam along pressed edge. Topstitch centrally along strip and neaten each end.

13 ◆ Turn under ends of Belt Loops and position Belt Loops directly over side seams, with lower end of Loop 60cm (23½in) above hem edge. Stitch Belt Loops in place by stitching across each end. Thread Belt through Belt Loops.

Variations on a Theme

These three easy-fitting tops are all based on the same boxy shape,
with the curved edges finished with bias strips.

1.10m (1¼yd) of 150cm (60in) wide fabric with or without nap

60cm (⅔yd) of 90cm (36in) wide iron-on interfacing

5 buttons

Matching thread

Scoop-neck top
1.10m (1¼yd) of 150cm (60in) wide fabric with or without nap

Matching thread

Vest top
70cm (¾yd) of 150cm (60in) wide fabric with or without nap

Matching thread

YOU COULD USE

Any light- to medium-weight fabric, such as the plain and printed crêpe de Chine used here, cotton or seersucker

SIZES

To fit size 10, 12–14 or 16

Finished length from nape of neck (all tops) 60cm (23½in)

MAKING PATTERN

Following Pattern Diagram on page 68, draw out pattern pieces full size – one square represents 5cm (2in). Hem allowance of 3cm (1¼in) and seam allowances of 1.5cm (⅝in) are included throughout. Transfer all pattern markings onto pattern pieces. For Scoop Neck Top, trim away back neck section to line indicated. For Vest Top, trim away front and back neck and armhole sections to lines indicated.

ADJUSTING THE SIZE

Pattern given is for size 12–14. To adjust size, cut through Front and Back pattern pieces along dotted line. For size 10, overlap pieces by 1.5cm (⅝in). For size 16, insert a strip of paper 1.5cm (⅝in) wide. Re-draw shoulder and hem cutting lines.

CUTTING OUT

Button-through top
Fold fabric in half lengthwise, with right sides facing, and pin pattern pieces to fabric following Layout Diagram on page 68. Cut out all pieces and transfer pattern markings onto fabric.
From fabric: Front – cut 2; Back – cut one to fold; Sleeve – cut 2. From remaining fabric, cut and join 4cm (1½in) wide bias strips (see page 53) to form one strip 70cm (27in) long.
From interfacing: Front – cut 2, cutting to marked fold line.

Scoop-neck top
Fold fabric in half lengthwise, with right sides facing, and pin Sleeve pattern piece to fabric. Cut out Sleeve. Now re-fold remaining fabric, with right sides facing, so that selvedges meet centrally along length and there are folds along both long edges. Pin Front and Back pattern pieces to fabric. Cut out these pieces. Transfer pattern markings onto all pieces. **From fabric, cut:** Front (cut one to fold), Back (cut one to fold), and Sleeve (cut 2). From remaining fabric, cut and join 4cm (1½in) wide bias strips (see page 53) to form one strip 90cm (36in) long.

Vest top
Fold fabric, with right sides facing, so that selvedges meet centrally along length and there are folds along both long edges. Pin Front and Back pattern pieces to fabric. Cut out these pieces. Transfer pattern markings onto all pieces. **From fabric, cut:** Front (cut one to fold), and Back (cut one to fold). From remaining fabric, cut and join 4cm (1½in) wide bias strips (see page 53) to form one strip 220cm (87in) long.

MAKING UP

All seams are stitched with right sides facing and then are pressed open unless stated otherwise.

Button-through top
1 ◆ Apply iron-on interfacing to wrong side of self-facings of Fronts. Neaten long straight edge of each facing. Stitch Fronts to Back across both shoulder seams and then press.
2 ◆ Fold facings to right side along marked fold line and baste in place at neck edge. Lay bias strip over ends of facings and along right side of neck edge, with raw edges level. Stitch entire neck seam. Trim seam, snip into seam allowance along curves and turn

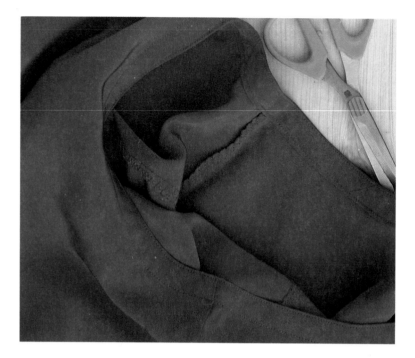

facings and bias strip to wrong side. Press, pressing facing to wrong side along front opening edge fold line. Fold 1cm (⅜in) to wrong side along remaining free edge of bias strip and baste in place. From right side, topstitch entire neck edge close to and 1.2cm (½in) from finished edge.

3 ◆ Stitch side seams and press.

4 ◆ Open out facings at hem edge. Fold 3cm (1¼in) hem allowance to wrong side along entire hem edge. Turn under raw edge and stitch in place. Press. Re-fold facings to wrong side and slip-stitch to hem allowance.

5 ◆ Stitch Sleeve seams and press. Matching underarm seams, notches, and sleeve dot to shoulder seam, stitch Sleeves into armholes (see page 41). Press seam towards Sleeve.

6 ◆ Fold 3 cm (1¼in) hem allowance to wrong side along lower edge of Sleeves and turn under raw edge. Stitch in place and press.

7 ◆ Make 5 horizontal buttonholes (see page 37) in right front. Position ends of buttonholes 1.2cm (½in) in from front opening edge, top buttonhole 1.5cm (⅝in) below corner where front neck slope begins, and remaining 4 buttonholes 7.5cm (3in) apart. Attach buttons to left front to correspond (see page 37).

Scoop-neck top

1 ◆ Stitch Front to Back across shoulder seams and press. Cut length of bias strip to fit neck seamline, allowing 3cm (1¼in) for join. Join ends to form a loop and press.

2 ◆ Taking 1.5cm (⅝in) seam and with right sides together, stitch bias strip to neck edge. Trim seam to 1cm (⅜in). Fold bias strip to inside, folding along seamline, and turn under 1cm (⅜in) along remaining raw edge of bias strip. Topstitch binding in place by stitching through all layers close to and 1.2cm (½in) from neck edge.

3 ◆ Make as for Button-through top, steps 3, 5 and 6.

4 ◆ Fold 3cm (1¼in) hem allowance to wrong side along entire hem edge of body section. Turn under raw edge and stitch in place. Press.

Vest top

1 ◆ Stitch Front to Back along shoulder and side seams and press.

2 ◆ Cut and join bias strip to form a loop to fit neck edge. With right sides facing, stitch bias strips to neck edge, taking 1cm (⅜in) seam. Press seam towards bias strip. Fold 1cm (⅜in) to wrong side along remaining free edge of bias strip and bring this folded edge over to wrong side to meet stitching line. Baste in place. From right side, topstitch bias strip in place by stitching through all layers 2mm (¹⁄₁₂in) from seamline. Press.

3 ◆ Attach bias strips to armhole edges in same way as for neck edge.

4 ◆ Fold 3cm (1¼in) hem allowance to wrong side along entire hem edge of body section. Turn under raw edge and stitch in place. Press.

Fastenings

*Fastenings are obviously a fundamental part of
most garments, so knowing how to insert a zip, make
buttonholes and sew on buttons and other fastenings is an
essential dressmaking skill.*

Zip fastenings

Most skirts, and many dresses, fasten with a
zip and, if this is inserted badly, it can easily
spoil the finished look of an otherwise
excellent garment. Zips are usually inserted
into an opening in a seam, and they can be centred
behind the seamline or set to one side. The latter

method is more suited to skirts and close-
fitting garments and is slightly easier to do.
However, the symmetrical stitching of the
centred zip makes it well-suited to centre
front and centre back positions. Wherever
the zip is to be placed, correct preparation of the
opening is important. Sew the seam that the zip is to

INSERTING A LAPPED ZIP

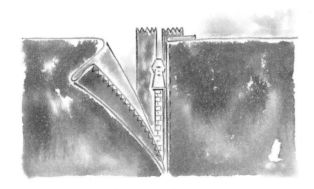

1 ◆ Remove the basting that holds the zip opening
closed. Place the zip under the righthand edge of the
opening so the pressed edge lies next to the zip
teeth; the zip stop should be positioned just above
the base of the opening. Pin and baste the zip in
place along this edge. Stitching from the right side,
with the zipper foot attachment on the machine,
stitch this side of the zip in place, as close as possible
to the zip opening edge. Fasten off securely.

2 ◆ Now bring the other edge of the zip opening over
the zip so that this free pressed edge just covers the
first line of stitching. Pin and baste the zip into
position along the lefthand edge. Now stitch this side
of the zip in place, stitching 1–1.2cm (⅜–½in) from
the pressed edge. Remember to stitch across the
base of the opening to the seamline.

be inserted into, leaving an opening that is slightly longer than the zip. Remember to fasten off securely at what will be the base of the opening. Now baste the remaining section of the seam closed, exactly along the seamline. Neaten the seam and press it open, taking care not to stretch the basted section.

Insert the zip using one of the methods shown on these pages. Use the zipper foot on your sewing machine – it can be moved from side to side, depending upon which side the zip teeth are on when you are stitching. Do not trim off the zip tapes at the bottom of the zip. Once complete, carefully press the zip opening, taking care not to create indentations of the zip teeth on the right side of the garment.

A **centred zip** has two lines of stitching which are equal distances from the actual opening edge. The zip teeth lie directly under the opening edge.

With a **lapped zip**, there is really only one visible line of stitching and the zip teeth are centred between this stitching line and the pressed edge of the zip opening. The two lines of stitching that hold the zip in place are done separately and should be stitched in the same direction – either from top to bottom or vice-versa.

INSERTING A CENTRED ZIP

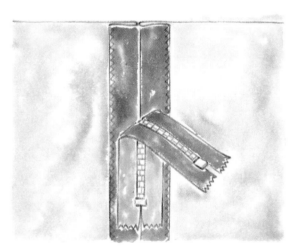

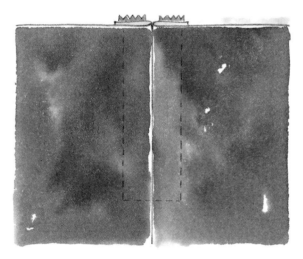

1 ◆ With the zip opening still basted closed, lay the closed zip against the wrong side of the fabric. The zip teeth should be directly over the basted seam and the zip stop at the lower edge just above the end of the machine stitching. The slider of the closed zip should be about 2.5cm (1in) from the top of the opening. Insert the pins at right angles to the zip. Now, working from the right side, baste the zip in place, working two parallel lines, one down each side of the zip to serve as stitching guidelines.

2 ◆ From the right side, and using a zipper foot attachment on your machine, stitch the zip in place. Start at the top of the lefthand edge and stitch 6–8mm (¼–⅜in) away from the basted seamline. At the base of the opening, just below the zip stop, stop stitching with the needle in the fabric, raise the machine foot and swing the fabric so that you can stitch across the base of the opening. Now swing the fabric again and complete the zip insertion by stitching along the righthand edge of the opening, stitching the same distance away from the basted seamline as before. Remove basting.

Buttonholes and buttons

Buttonholes should be marked very carefully and stitched accurately. If a buttonhole is placed on a band, it should run parallel to the longer edges of the band, not across it. It – and the button it will fasten over – should also be placed centrally across the band.

Many sewing machine manuals will tell you the best way to sew a buttonhole using that particular machine. A buttonhole is basically two rows of very short, narrow zigzag stitches worked next to each other, with wider zigzag stitches worked across each end. To achieve a buttonhole that is really even, loosen the tension of the top thread slightly so that the stitches interlock just to the wrong side of the work, leaving the right side neat.

A buttonhole should be slightly longer than the button that is to pass through it. About 1–2mm ($\frac{1}{24}$–$\frac{1}{12}$in) longer is sufficient, unless you are using a very thick button, where it may need to be slightly longer still. Take great care when cutting the buttonhole that you do not accidentally cut through the stitching. The two rows of stitching forming the sides of the buttonhole should be just far enough apart to allow you to cut between them. Use small, very sharp scissors to cut the buttonhole after it has been sewn. Stop cutting just before you get to the end stitches.

When a button is attached it should stand just above the surface of the garment. That way, once the garment is buttoned, the button will lie flat against this second section without distorting it.

Hooks and eyes

Hooks and eyes are often used to fasten waistbands and neck edges. Those with loop-shaped eyes are used where there is no overlap, and those with bar-shaped eyes where there is an overlap. The hook and eye are sewn on by hand using a double-thread. Position the hook on the wrong side with the end even with the garment edge.

A loop-shaped eye is positioned on the wrong side of the garment, opposite the hook, with the end protruding beyond the garment edge just enough to allow it to be fastened. A bar-shaped eye is sewn to the right side of the underlap.

MAKING A BUTTONHOLE

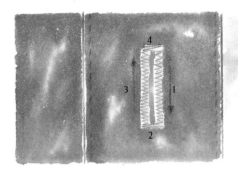

♦ To make a buttonhole, start by working the first side forwards, then work one end set of stitches. Next, the second side is usually worked in reverse, ending with the second set of wider stitches. If your machine will not work the reverse stitches as evenly as the first side, then work this side forwards as well by turning the work at the first end of the buttonhole.

ATTACHING A BUTTON

♦ Start by sewing on the button using a double thickness of sewing thread and leaving all the stitches slightly loose. You may find it easier to do this if you slip a matchstick between the button and the fabric. Once the button is attached, wind the remaining thread tightly around the shank of threads created. Work one or two stitches through this shank and cut off the thread.

Skirting the Issue

Whether you want a neat mini or a sophisticated long line,
these slim-fitting tailored skirts are classics.

YOU WILL NEED

150cm (60in) wide fabric with or without nap

Long skirt: 1.05m (1¼yd)

Short skirt: 75cm (⅞yd)

Both skirts

10cm (⅛yd) of 90cm (36in) wide iron-on interfacing

18cm (7in) zip

1 button

Matching thread

YOU COULD USE

Any medium- to heavy-weight fabric, such as the bouclé tweed used here

SIZES

To fit size 10, 12, 14 or 16

Long skirt: finished length from waist 80cm (31½in)

Short skirt: finished length from waist 50cm (19¾in)

MAKING PATTERN

Following Long or Short Skirt Pattern and Layout Diagram on page 67, draw out pattern pieces full size – one square represents 5cm (2in). Hem allowance of 5cm (2in) and seam allowances of 1.5cm (⅝in) are included throughout. For Short Skirt, trim away lower and back pleat sections of Front and Back pattern pieces as marked by dashed lines. Transfer pattern markings onto pattern pieces.

ADJUSTING THE SIZE

Pattern given is for size 12. To adjust size, cut through Front and Back pattern pieces along dotted line. For size 10, overlap pieces by 1.25cm (½in). For size 14, insert a strip of paper 1.25cm (½in) wide. For size 16, insert a strip of paper 2.5cm (1in) wide. Re-draw waist and hem cutting lines. For size 10, trim 2.5cm (1in) from waistband. For size 14, add 2.5cm (1in) to waistband, and for size 16 add 5cm (2in) to waistband.

CUTTING OUT

Fold fabric in half lengthwise, with right sides facing, and pin pattern pieces to fabric following Pattern and Layout Diagram. Cut out all pieces and transfer pattern markings onto fabric.

From fabric (Long or Short Skirt): Front – cut one to fold; Back – cut 2; Waistband – cut one to fold.

From interfacing: Waistband – cut one to fold.

MAKING UP

All seams are stitched with right sides facing then are pressed open unless stated otherwise.

Long skirt

1 ◆ Stitch darts in Front and Back and press away from side seams.

2 ◆ Neaten inner edge of pleat allowance of Right Back along pleat opening edge parallel to fold line. Fold 6mm (¼in) to wrong side along this edge and stitch in place. Stitch Backs together along centre back seam, leaving seam open for zip above upper dot and pivoting stitching at corner dot, stitching across top of pleat. Baste pleat in place along fold line indicated on pattern below corner dot. Neaten seam and opening edges. Press seam open, pleat towards Left Back and seam allowances to wrong side along zip opening edges. Topstitch through all layers between dots and along marked stitching line.

3 ◆ Insert zip into centre back opening and press.

4 ◆ Stitch Front to Backs along side seam edges and press open.

Press seam towards Waistband, and seam allowance to wrong side along other long edge.

6 ◆ Fold Waistband in half with right sides together and stitch across Left Back end. At Right Back end, stitch across end and along to meet end of Waistband stitching. Trim seam and corners and turn right side out.

7 ◆ Position pressed edge of Waistband level with stitching line on inside and hand stitch in place. Press.

8 ◆ Release pleat basting and unfold pleat at hem edge. Neaten hem edge. Fold 5cm (2in) to wrong side and stitch in place. Refold pleat and hand stitch pleat allowance to hem allowance on inside. Press.

9 ◆ Make buttonhole centrally along left back end of Waistband, positioning end of buttonhole 1cm (⅜in) from end of Waistband. Attach button to other end of Waistband to correspond.

Short skirt

1 ◆ Make as for Long Skirt, step 1.

2 ◆ Stitch Backs together along centre back seam, leaving seam open for zip above upper dot. Neaten seam and opening edges. Press seam open and seam allowances to wrong side along zip opening edges.

3 ◆ Insert zip into centre back opening and press.

4 ◆ Make as for Long skirt, steps 4 to 7.

5 ◆ Neaten hem edge. Fold 5cm (2in) to wrong side and stitch in place. Press.

6 ◆ Make as for Long Skirt, step 9.

5 ◆ Apply interfacing to wrong side of Waistband. Pin one long edge of Waistband to upper edge of skirt – position one end of Waistband 4.5cm (1¾in) beyond zip opening edge of Right Back and other end of Waistband 1.5cm (⅝in) beyond zip opening edge of Left Back. Stitch Waistband in place. Snip to end of stitching at Right Back end, and snip into seam allowance to stitching point 4.5cm (1¾in) from this end of Waistband along other long edge.

Making Shirts

A professional-looking shirt is not difficult to make,
provided you follow basic guidelines for the collar, cuffs, sleeves
and other important aspects.

Collars and cuffs

Collars and cuffs (and waistbands too, incidentally) are really just glorified bands and are usually attached as such (see pages 24 and 26). The easiest collars to make are those which lie flat against the neck edge of the garment. Another type rises up from the neckline and then turns down, forming a rolled edge around the neck. A third type, often found in tailored shirts, has a stand; sometimes the stand is a separate section encasing the collar, while at other times it is an extension of the collar piece.

For collars and cuffs (and waistbands) to hold their shape, they *must* be interfaced. If you are using a very lightweight fabric, you could use a second layer of the main fabric, or lining fabric, instead. If you are using an iron-on interfacing, always apply it to the section that will not show (on collars this is known as the undercollar) in case the glue shows through the fabric.

After stitching the collar or cuff pieces together, you need to layer, or **grade**, the seam allowance. Trim the interfacing close to the stitching, then trim the undercollar or cuff seam allowance to 3mm (⅛in) and the collar or cuff seam allowance to 6mm (¼in) to prevent a ridge. Snip off the points within the seam allowance of a cuff or pointed collar, and clip the curves of a rounded collar, then turn right side out.

Any problems that arise in making collars are usually due to the shapes of the edges you are sewing together. Although the actual seamlines that are to be joined will be the same length, the cut neck edge will usually be much shorter, as it is generally on a curve. To make it easier to sew the collar to the body, machine stitch along the neck edge just within the seam allowance. You can then snip into the seam allowance (but being very careful not into the stitching) so that the edge will open out, allowing you to sew it to the collar edge much more easily.

Inserting a sleeve

The way a sleeve is inserted can affect the entire look of the garment, especially as it usually involves smoothly easing in some fullness. There are two main types of sleeve, the standard set-in sleeve, and the shirt sleeve.

Set-in sleeves are almost completed before being sewn into the armholes. This type of sleeve usually has quite a lot of fullness over the sleevehead and, unless you want unsightly gathers, this fullness must be eased into the armhole edge.

Shirt sleeves are attached to the body section of the garment before the side seams and sleeve seams are stitched. They are actually inserted in virtually the same way as set-in sleeves, but are easier to do because you are working with two flat pieces of fabric, rather than sewing a tube into a hole. Also, there is usually less fullness to ease in. The gathering threads are run along exactly the same section of the sleevehead as for a set-in sleeve (see opposite, step 1), the sleeve is pinned and basted in place, and then the armhole is stitched with the wrong side of the sleeve uppermost. Once the armhole seam is stitched, the side seam and sleeve seam can be sewn in one continuous operation.

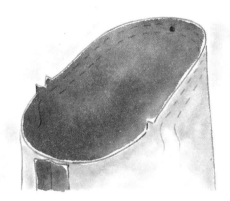

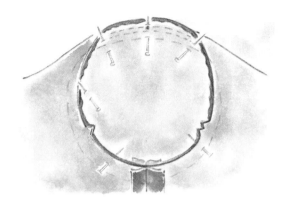

1 ◆ Most of the fullness in a set-in sleeve is between the notches on each side of the dot that marks the top of the sleevehead (the one you will match to the shoulder seam). To ease in the fullness, run gathering threads just inside and just outside the sleevehead seamline, starting and ending at points about a third of the way up from the underarm seam. This procedure is known as ease-stitching.

2 ◆ Turn the sleeve right side out and the garment wrong side out. Pin the sleeve into the armhole, matching all the relevant dots, seams and notches, and carefully pulling up the gathering threads so that all the fullness is eased in smoothly. Baste the sleeve in place.

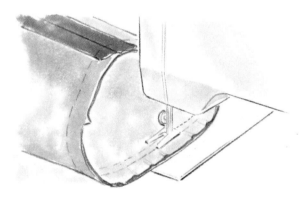

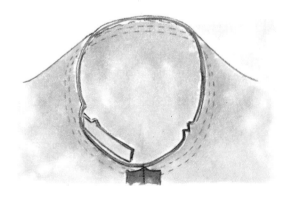

3 ◆ Now stitch the armhole seam, working with the wrong side of the sleeve uppermost and starting and stopping at the underarm point. Stitch again alongside the first row of stitching 6mm (¼in) inside the seam allowance.

4 ◆ Remove all the basting and gathering threads. There should be no little pleats of extra fabric anywhere along the seam. If there are, unpick this section of the seam and re-stitch it, making sure it is smooth this time. To reduce bulk, trim the seam to about 6mm (¼in) for 10–12cm (4–4¾in) either side of the underarm point.

Flat-fell seams

One hallmark of a really professionally made shirt is its flat-fell seams. These are like the seams you find down the legs of a pair of jeans. They are much more hardwearing than normal seams and are quite quick to make (see below), as the edges are actually neatened as the seam is stitched.

Working with checked fabrics

Ideally, when a checked fabric is sewn together to form a shirt or other garment, the checks should all match. However, as the shapes of the garment pieces rarely allow this to happen both horizontally and vertically, make sure that the checks at least match horizontally. To ensure this happens, care must be taken both when cutting out and when seaming.

When cutting out a checked fabric, try to position the final hem line midway through a wide band of the check. That way, if the edge is slightly curved, the hem line will not be cutting in and out of the stripes that form the check effect.

Ensure that the checks will match up from one section to another by checking that the notches positioned along vertical seams fall at the same point in a pattern repeat on all sections. As it is usually impossible to fold checked fabric so that the checks are identically placed on both layers, cut out the pieces first through the top layer of fabric only. Fold back the scraps and pin these cut pieces onto the other layer, matching the checks exactly, before you cut the second piece.

Take care when seaming the pieces together that you do not stretch or otherwise distort the fabric, thereby causing the checks no longer to match – time spent pinning and basting here will be well worth it when you view your finished garment!

MAKING A FLAT-FELL SEAM

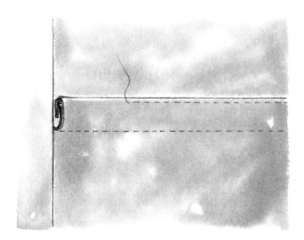

♦ Start by making a normal seam, stitching it with the right sides together. Decide which side of the seam the flat-fell seam is to lie on, and trim away half the seam allowance along the edge at this side. Now fold the remaining raw edge over this trimmed edge to enclose it. Complete the seam by stitching the new folded edge in place to the garment.

♦ A flat-fell seam made in this way will have a row of stitching visible on the right side that runs parallel to the seam line. On the wrong side, there are two rows of stitching visible. If you prefer this effect then stitch the initial seam with the wrong sides together.

BIG IDEAS

*This generously cut overshirt has a stand-up
collar, sleeves with cuffs, a breast pocket and buttonholes – all of
which are within the capabilities of a beginner.*

YOU WILL NEED

2m (2¼yd) of 150cm (60in)
wide fabric without nap

80cm (⅞yd) of 90cm (36in)
wide iron-on interfacing

8 buttons

Matching thread

YOU COULD USE

Any light- to medium-
weight fabric, such as the
checked cotton used here,
poplin or crêpe de Chine

SIZES

To fit size 10–12 or 14–16

Finished length from back
neck 79cm (31in)

MAKING PATTERN

Following Pattern and Layout Diagram on page 68, draw out pattern
pieces full size – one square
represents 5cm (2in). Hem
allowance of 2.5cm (1in) and
seam allowances of 1.5cm (⅝in)
are included throughout.
Transfer all pattern markings
onto pattern pieces.

ADJUSTING THE SIZE

Pattern given is for size 10–12. To
adjust for size 14–16, cut through
Front and Back pattern pieces
along dotted line and insert a
strip of paper 2.5cm (1in) wide.
Re-draw shoulder and hem
cutting lines.

CUTTING OUT

Fold fabric in half lengthwise, with
right sides facing, and pin pattern
pieces to fabric following Pattern
and Layout Diagram. Cut out all
pieces and transfer pattern markings onto fabric.
From fabric: Front – cut 2; Back –
cut one to fold; Pocket – cut one;
Collar Stand – cut 2; Collar – cut
2; Sleeve – cut 2; Cuff – cut 2; Cuff
Opening Facing – cut 2.
From interfacing: Front – cut 2,
cutting to marked fold line; Collar
Stand – cut one; Collar – cut one;
Cuff – cut 2.

MAKING UP

All seams are stitched with right
sides facing then are pressed
open unless stated otherwise.
1 ◆ Apply interfacing to wrong
sides of self-facings along front
opening edges of Fronts against
fold line. Fold 5cm (2in) to wrong

side along this edge and turn
under 1.5cm (⅝in) along raw
edge. Stitch in place close to both
folded edges, and again 6mm
(¼in) from folded edges. Press.
2 ◆ Neaten side and lower edges
of Pocket. Press 6mm (¼in) to
wrong side across opening edge.
Fold self-facing to right side
across top of Pocket along fold
line indicated on pattern and
stitch across ends of facing. Turn
facing to wrong side and press,
pressing seam allowances to
wrong side along remaining
edges. Topstitch facing in place by
stitching close to lower pressed
edge and again 6mm (¼in) from
upper edge.
3 ◆ Place Pocket onto right side of
Left Front 14cm (5½in) in from
front opening edge and with
opening edge of Pocket 58cm
(22¾in) above hem edge of Front.
Topstitch Pocket in position close
to lower and side edges and again
6mm (¼in) from edges. Press.
4 ◆ Stitch Back to Front along
shoulder seams and press.
5 ◆ Apply interfacing to wrong
side of one Collar piece. Stitch
Collar pieces together along
straight edges. Trim seam and
corners and turn Collar through to

right side. Press, positioning seam along pressed edge. Top-stitch seamed edges close to and 6mm (¼in) from edges. Press.

6 ◆ Apply interfacing to wrong side of one Collar Stand piece. Press seam allowance to wrong side along neck edge of this section. Matching dots, pin Collar to right side of this Collar Stand piece, with interfaced Collar section against Collar Stand. Lay other Collar Stand piece over these, matching seamlines, and stitch pieces together. Trim and snip into seam allowances and turn Collar Stand through to right side. Press, pressing Collar away from Collar Stand.

7 ◆ With right sides facing, stitch uninterfaced Collar Stand section to neck edge of body. Trim and snip into seam allowances and press seam toward Collar Stand. Bring pressed edge of interfaced Collar Stand over seam to match stitching line and slip-stitch in place. Topstitch close to and 6mm (¼in) from all edges of Collar Stand. Press.

8 ◆ Fold 6mm (¼in) to wrong side along upper and side edges of Cuff Opening Facing. With right sides together, lay Cuff Opening Facing over Sleeve, matching cutting lines and dots, and stitch pieces together 6mm (¼in) from cutting line, tapering in to nothing and pivoting stitching at dot. Cut centrally between stitching to dot and fold Facing to wrong side. Press. Topstitch Facing in place close to pressed outer edges and seamed opening edges. Press.

9 ◆ Baste darts in cuff edge of Sleeve and press away from cuff opening. Matching Sleeve dot to shoulder seam and with cuff opening section of Sleeve to back of body sections, stitch Sleeve to body. Press seam towards Sleeve.

10 ◆ Matching armhole seams and dots, stitch side and sleeve seams in one operation, leaving side seam open below dot. Press, pressing seam allowances to wrong side along side seam opening edges below dots. Turn under raw edges along side seam openings and topstitch in place close to inner folded edges.

11 ◆ Apply interfacing to wrong side of Cuff. Pin one long edge of Cuff to lower edge of Sleeve. Position one end of Cuff 4.5cm (1¾in) beyond cuff opening edge nearest sleeve seam and other end of Cuff 1.5cm (⅝in) beyond cuff opening edge nearest darts. Stitch Cuff in place. Snip to end of stitching at sleeve seam end, and snip into seam allowance to

stitching point 4.5cm (1¾in) from this end of Cuff along other long edge. Press seam towards Cuff, and seam allowance to wrong side along other long edge of Cuff.

12 ◆ Fold Cuff in half with right sides together and stitch across end nearest darts. At sleeve seam end, stitch across end and along to meet end of Cuff stitching. Trim seam and corners and turn Cuff ends through to right side.

13 ◆ Position pressed edge of Cuff level with stitching line on inside and slip-stitch in place. Press. Remove dart tacking. Topstitch close to and 6mm (¼in) from all edges of Cuff. Press.

14 ◆ Fold 2.5cm (1in) hem allowance to wrong side along lower edges of Fronts and Back. Turn under raw edge and baste in place. Topstitch hem in place close to upper folded edge and again 6mm (¼in) away from edge. Press.

15 ◆ Make horizontal buttonhole centrally along end of Cuff nearest darts – position end of buttonhole 1.5cm (⅝in) from end of Cuff. Attach button to other end of Cuff to correspond.

16 ◆ Make horizontal buttonhole centrally along right front end of Collar Stand – position end of buttonhole 1.5cm (⅝in) from end of Collar Stand. Make a further 5 vertical buttonholes in Right Front centrally between lines of topstitching; position centre of top buttonhole 8.5cm (3¼in) below buttonhole in Collar Stand and space remaining buttonholes 10cm (4in) apart. Attach buttons to Left Front to correspond.

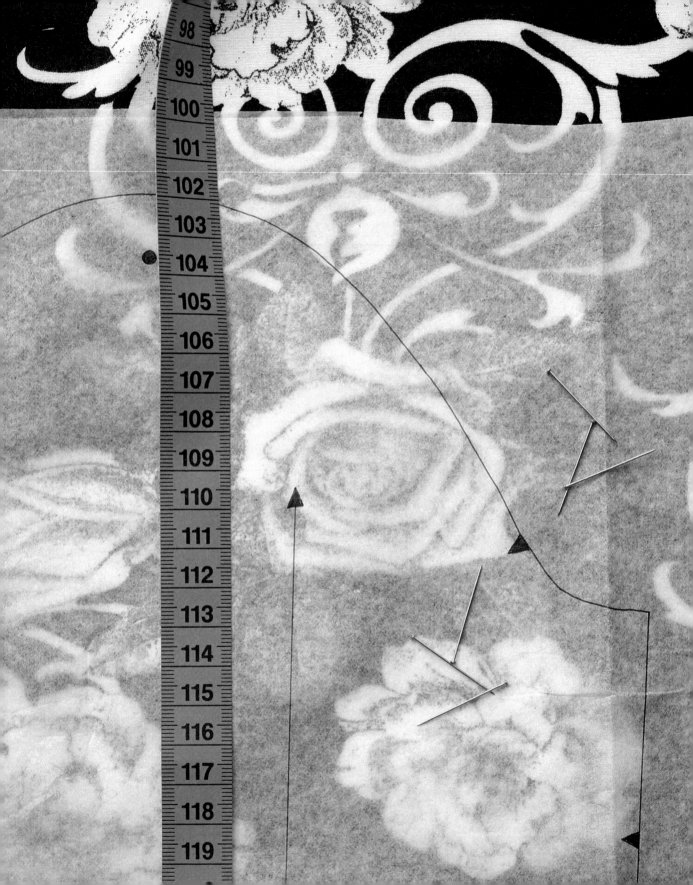

Special Fabrics

Certain types of fabric require
special handling – but this does not mean they are difficult
to use if you know what to do.

Large prints and border prints
The special handling that these fabrics require involves the way in which they are cut out. A **large-print** fabric should obviously be treated as a with-nap fabric unless you are one hundred per cent sure it is not! A **border-print** fabric has a design on it that will form a border along one selvedge. Therefore, the grain has to run horizontally across the garment. If the pattern you have chosen is designed for use with a border-print fabric, the grain line marked on the pattern pieces will allow for this. If, however, you have chosen to use a pattern that was not specifically designed for that type of fabric, you will need to draw in new grain lines on your pattern pieces – these should be placed at right angles to the existing ones. When laying out the pattern pieces, try to match the motif at the side seams.

CUTTING OUT LARGE PRINTS AND BORDER-PRINT FABRICS

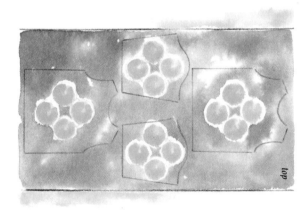

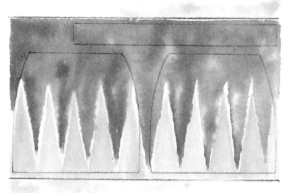

♦ When cutting out **large-print** fabrics, try to position the pattern pieces so that the focal point of the print falls in the middle of a section. Also, try to match up the positioning of the design on the front and back and, if possible, the sleeves.

♦ Normally, when cutting out fabric, you would have the grain running vertically along the body – but a **border print** fabric is different. Because of the nature of the design, you must have the grain of the fabric running horizontally across the body.

Panel prints

Panel prints will basically break all the rules when you cut them out. If the pattern has been specifically designed for use with that type of fabric, you will find details of exactly how the pattern pieces should be positioned. If it has not, you must decide for yourself exactly how you are going to place the pieces on the fabric. Bear in mind, though, that you will lose a certain amount of the print in the seam and hem allowances and that, if your garment is to hang correctly, you need to have the grain of the fabric running either vertically or horizontally across the body. If you are unable to buy a panel-print fabric, you could use head scarves. After all, that is basically what a panel print is.

Very light-weight and transparent fabrics

The way these fabrics are seamed and the type of interfacing which should be used are the main factors that will determine whether your garment looks as good as it should.

Take great care to use the correct weight of **interfacing** – otherwise, a fluid garment could have areas that stand out like a board. It is best to try to avoid iron-on interfacing, as the glue may show through, or there may be a noticeable line from the right side along the edge of the interfacing. If you do decide to use an iron-on interfacing, make sure it is applied to the facing sections, not the outer sections. If you are unable to buy the correct weight of interfacing, use a cotton lawn or lining fabric instead. This will help retain the soft look of your fabric.

It is more the way the seams are finished than the way they are sewn that will affect the finished garment. If the fabric is very fine and transparent, leaving a 1.5cm (⅝in) seam allowance that is neatened and pressed open may spoil the look of what you are making. Try trimming both seam allowances to 6mm (¼in) and neatening the raw edges together. Press this seam to one side – usually the back or downwards – and you will find that the seam is much less noticeable from the right side.

Another good way to join fine or transparent fabrics is by making a **French seam**. This type of seam is stitched in two stages and as a result the raw edges are totally enclosed.

MAKING A FRENCH SEAM

1 ◆ Start by stitching the seam in the normal way – but have the *wrong* sides together and take only just under half the stated seam allowance. Trim the seam allowance back to within 3–4mm (⅛in) of the stitching line and press it open.

2 ◆ Now fold the sections along the first seamline with right sides together and stitch the seam again, stitching along the actual seamline. Press this seam to one side. You will see that all the raw edges are totally enclosed within the seam.

Jersey or knitted fabrics

It is because of their stretchiness that jersey or knitted fabrics require careful handling at certain stages in their use.

Because of the way these fabrics are made, they will usually stretch easily – and if a tiny hole is stretched, it will quickly ladder! It is therefore important that anything that pierces through the fabric does not break the fibres – if it does, a hole will appear that could ladder as soon as the fabric is stretched at all.

If you are working with a jersey fabric, make sure you use a machine needle which is designed for use with a knitted fabric. These are sometimes called perfect-stitch or ballpoint needles. They have smooth, rounded tips that separate the fibres of the fabric as they pierce through, rather than simply pushing straight through the fibres and possibly breaking them.

It is possible to buy ballpoint pins and hand-sewing needles; but, if care is taken with ordinary pins and needles and any damaged ones are rejected, this is not usually necessary.

As some jersey fabrics stretch quite easily, care must be taken when cutting them out that the fabric is not stretched or distorted out of shape. If it is, the final garment may appear distorted and will not hang correctly. Be careful to place all pattern pieces on the correct grain, otherwise you may find that your garment stretches in places you don't want it to!

Obviously if the garment is to stretch, the seams must stretch too. To sew them, use a synthetic thread, which has a little 'give' in it and is therefore less likely to break.

Try to use a narrow, short zigzag stitch for all the seaming. This will give the seams the amount of stretch they need without causing the seam to break. Use a stitch width of about 1.5mm (1/16in) and a stitch length to suit the weight of the fabric.

Even though it may appear rather difficult to press a zigzagged seam flat, it will actually press just as flat as a straight-stitched seam. If you need to work decorative topstitching with a straight stitch, use a stitch length shorter than you would normally – this will give a little extra stretch to the stitching.

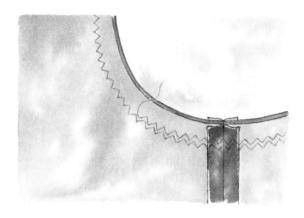

◆ It is a good idea to work a second line of stitching just inside the first line in areas where the seam may be under pressure – such as the crotch seam on leggings or trousers. Position this second line 1–2mm (1/24–1/12in) away from the first, within seam allowance.

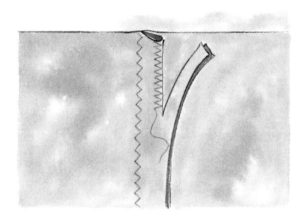

◆ One good feature of jersey fabrics is that they do not usually fray, so there is no real need to neaten the edges. However, as light-weight jersey has a tendency to roll, it is a good idea to trim both seam allowances to 6–10mm (1/4–3/8in) and then neaten both raw edges together with a wide zigzag stitch. This will help to keep the seam flat.

THE WEAR WITH ALL

*Knowing how to work with
stretch fabrics makes it possible to sew your
own leggings, which these days are a wardrobe essential. They
are so quick and easy, you could make
any number of them!*

YOU WILL NEED

1.70m (1⅞yd) of 90cm (36in) wide stretch jersey fabric without nap

Waist length of 2.5cm (1in) wide elastic

Matching thread

YOU COULD USE

Any medium- to heavy-weight stretch jersey fabric, such as the marled cotton/Lycra jersey used here, cotton jersey or tracksuiting

Note: this pattern is unsuitable for non-stretch fabrics.

SIZES

To fit size 10, 12, 14 or 16

Finished length from waist 102cm (39¾in)

MAKING PATTERN

Following Pattern and Layout Diagram on page 70, draw out pattern pieces full size – one square represents 5cm (2in). Hem allowance of 3cm (1¼in), casing allowance of 4cm (1½in) and seam allowances of 1.5cm (⅝in) are included throughout. Transfer all pattern markings onto pattern pieces.

ADJUSTING THE SIZE

Pattern given is for size 12. To adjust size, cut through pattern pieces along dotted line. For size 10, overlap pieces by 1.25cm (½in). For size 14, insert a strip of paper 1.25cm (½in) wide. For size 16, insert a strip of paper 2.5cm (1in) wide. Re-draw waist and hem cutting lines.

CUTTING OUT

Fold fabric in half lengthwise, with right sides facing, and pin pattern pieces to fabric following Pattern and Layout Diagram. Cut out all pieces and transfer pattern markings onto fabric.

From fabric: Front – cut 2; Back – cut 2.

MAKING UP

All seams are stitched with right sides facing using a narrow, short zigzag stitch. Trim seam allowances to 1cm (⅜in), neaten raw edges together and press seam to one side.

1 ◆ Matching notches, stitch Fronts and Backs along outside leg/side seam and inside leg seam. Trim and neaten seams and press towards back.

2 ◆ Turn one leg right side out and slip this leg inside the other so that right sides are facing. Matching waist edges and inside leg seams, stitch legs together along centre front and back crotch seams. Trim and neaten seam and press towards left leg.

3 ◆ Fold 4cm (1½in) casing allowance to wrong side around waist edge and turn under raw edge. Stitch casing in place close to both folded edges, leaving an opening in lower row of stitching to insert elastic. Press.

4 ◆ Cut length of elastic to fit waist, and thread it through casing. Join ends securely and stitch casing opening closed.

5 ◆ Fold 3cm (1¼in) hem allowance to wrong side around lower edge of each leg and turn under raw edge. Stitch hem in place close to both folded edges. Press.

Working on the Bias

*Although in the majority of garments
the grain of the fabric runs either vertically
or horizontally across the body, sometimes the pieces are cut
so that the grain runs diagonally across
the body – on the bias.*

Fabric cut on the bias has much more elasticity than when it is cut on the straight grain. The bias grain of a fabric runs diagonally to the true (straight) grain and it is along this line that a woven fabric will stretch. A pattern designed to be cut on the bias will have a grain line marked on it that relates to the true grain, which runs diagonally across the pattern pieces.

Bias-cut garments

Sometimes only some of the sections will be cut on the bias – a dress, for example, can have the bodice cut on the true grain and the skirt sections cut on the bias – and this is done to achieve a certain look. Sometimes the bias grain is used as a style feature, like bias-cut bands on a checked skirt. At other times, a bias-cut garment will have its facings cut on the straight, or true, grain. Straight-grain sections have less stretch and therefore help the outer sections to hold their correct shape.

An angle of exactly 45 degrees to the straight grain of the fabric is known as the 'true bias'. Not only does the true bias give maximum stretch, but it is also important if the fabric you are using is striped or checked or has a distinctive weave, since these won't look right otherwise. (Jersey fabric, however, would be *too* stretchy if cut on the true bias. It is therefore cut at an angle of a little less than 45 degrees, more generally known as 'on the bias'.)

As the bias grain of a fabric stretches far more than the true or crosswise grain, great care must be taken when cutting out and seaming the sections. If the fabric is distorted out of shape at either stage, the garment will not hang correctly. Garments cut on the bias will have a tendency to drop, or stretch, in wear and, as the fabric drops, the hem line can become uneven. It is a good idea to allow a bias-cut garment to hang on a suitable coat hanger for at least 24 hours before hemming it. During that time the fabric will sag and drop as much as it is likely to and you can then trim the hem edge level. This way, when you wear your garment, you can be fairly sure your level hem line will remain that way.

Self-fabric bias binding

As fabric cut on the bias stretches and moulds to a shape well, it makes an ideal binding for a curved edge. While purchased bias binding is widely available, you may wish to bind the edges of a garment with bias-cut strips of the actual garment fabric. Bias binding is generally cut on the true bias. Remember, however, that you may need to buy extra fabric to enable you to cut out these strips.

Self-fabric bias binding such as this is attached in exactly the same way as purchased bias binding. But, as the seamline creases are not pressed in place for you, take care to position correctly the raw edges of the pieces that are to be seamed together. It is possible to buy a gadget that allows you to press these creases in your own bias binding, and one of these may be worth investing in if you plan to sew a lot.

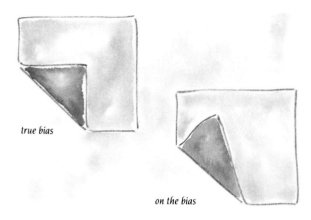

true bias

on the bias

1 ◆ To find the 'true bias', fold the corner of your fabric as shown, so that a crosswise thread lies exactly over a lengthwise thread. The fold will then be at an angle of precisely 45 degrees to the selvedge. To cut strips 'on the bias' rather than on the true bias, fold it at a shallower angle.

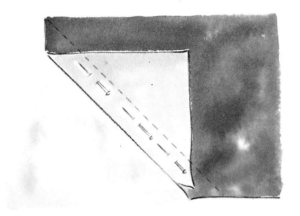

2 ◆ Put in a few pins parallel to the fold and a little distance away from it, to keep the fabric flat. Flatten the fabric against the table and carefully cut along the fold.

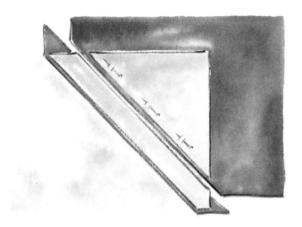

3 ◆ Cutting parallel to this first cut, cut out strips of the desired width, which should be four times the width of the finished binding, once again using pins to keep the fabric flat.

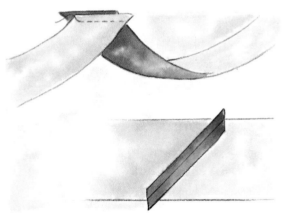

4 ◆ If you need to join lengths to achieve one long strip, stitch the ends together, right sides facing, on the straight grain and press the seams open. Getting the seam exactly on the straight grain and the long edges in line can be tricky, so be sure to pin and baste first.

Sweet Nothings

*The clinginess of fabric cut on
the bias makes it ideal for lingerie, as in this
camisole and petticoat. In fact, in a suitable fabric, the pattern
could just as well be used for a pretty
summer skirt and top.*

YOU WILL NEED

Camisole

80cm (⅞yd) of 115cm (45in)
wide fabric without nap

Matching thread

Petticoat

2m (2¼yd) of 115cm (45in)
wide fabric without nap

Matching thread

YOU COULD USE

Any light- to medium-
weight fabric, such as the
crêpe de Chine used here,
cotton lawn, fine satin,
satin-back crêpe or viscose

Note: This pattern is unsuitable for stretch fabrics.

SIZES

To fit size 10, 12, 14 or 16

Camisole: finished length
from underarm – 27cm
(10½in)

Petticoat: finished length
from underarm – 75cm
(29½in)

MAKING PATTERN

For size 12, fold pattern paper in half and, following Pattern Diagram on page 69, draw out pattern pieces full size, placing fold of pattern against fold of paper – one square represents 5cm (2in). Hem allowance of 1.5cm (⅝in) and seam allowances of 1.5cm (⅝in) are included throughout. For Front and Back Facings, trace off upper section of Front and Back above dashed lines; note that these pieces should have grain lines running *parallel* to the fold, not on the bias as for Front and Back. Transfer all pattern markings onto pattern pieces, and open out pattern pieces to full size.

For size 10, make pattern as for size 12 but position fold line on Back and Back Facing pattern pieces 1.25cm (½in) beyond fold of paper. For both Skirt sections, position fold of pattern 6mm (¼in) beyond fold of paper. For Front and Front Facing, cut along dotted line marked on pattern and overlap pattern pieces by 1.25cm (½in). Re-draw neck and hem cutting lines.

For size 14, make pattern as for size 12 but position fold line on Back and Back Facing pattern pieces 1.25cm (½in) away from fold of paper. For both Skirt sections, position fold of pattern 6mm (¼in) away from fold of paper. For Front and Front Facing, cut along dotted line marked on pattern and insert a strip of paper 1.25cm (½in) wide. Re-draw neck and hem cutting lines.

For size 16, make pattern as for size 12 but position fold line on Back and Back Facing pattern pieces 2.5cm (1in) away from fold of paper. For both Skirt sections, position fold of pattern 1.25cm (½in) away from fold of paper. For Front and Front Facing, cut along dotted line marked on pattern and insert a strip of paper 2.5cm (1in) wide. Re-draw neck and hem cutting lines.

CUTTING OUT

Lay fabric out flat, right side up, and pin pattern pieces to fabric following Layout Diagram on page 69. For Camisole, ignore Skirt sections. Cut out all pieces

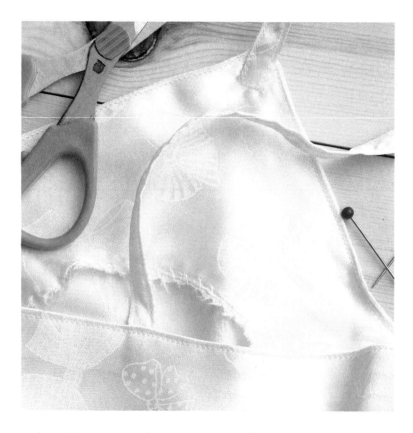

and transfer pattern markings onto fabric.

Camisole
From fabric: Front – cut one; Back – cut one; Front facing – cut one; Back Facing – cut one; Strap – cut 2.

Petticoat
From fabric: Front – cut one; Back – cut one; Front Facing – cut one; Back Facing – cut one; Strap – cut 2; Front Skirt – cut 2; Back Skirt – cut 2.

MAKING UP
All seams are stitched with right sides facing then are pressed open unless stated otherwise.

Camisole
1 ◆ Stitch darts in Front and press downwards. Stitch Front to Back along side seams. Trim seam allowance to 6mm (¼in), neaten raw edges together and press towards Back.

2 ◆ Stitch Front Facing to Back Facing along side seams and press. Neaten entire lower edge.

3 ◆ Fold each Strap in half lengthwise and stitch along length. Trim seam to 6mm (¼in) and turn Strap right side out. Press, placing seam along one pressed edge. Topstitch Straps close to both long edges. Pin one end of each Strap to upper edge of Back at position marked by dot and with

end of Strap level with upper edge of Back.

4 ◆ Stitch facings to upper edge of Front and Back, enclosing ends of Straps in seam. Trim seam and corners, snip along curves and turn facing to wrong side. Press, positioning seam along pressed edge. Topstitch close to upper edge.

5 ◆ Neaten remaining free ends of Straps and neatly hand sew ends to inside of Front Facing at top of points.

6 ◆ Fold 1.5cm (⅝in) hem allowance to wrong side around lower edge. Turn under raw edge and stitch in place. Press.

Petticoat
1 ◆ Make as for Camisole, steps 1 to 5.

2 ◆ Stitch Front Skirt pieces together along centre front seam, and Back Skirt pieces together along centre back seam. Trim seam to 6mm (¼in), neaten raw edges together and press to one side.

3 ◆ Stitch Front Skirt to Back Skirt along side seam edges. Trim seam to 6mm (¼in), neaten raw edges together and press seam allowance towards back.

4 ◆ Matching side seams and centre front and back points, stitch skirt sections to lower edge of bodice sections. Trim seam to 6mm (¼in), neaten raw edges together and press downwards.

5 ◆ Fold 1.5cm (⅝in) hem allowance to wrong side around lower edge of skirt sections. Turn under raw edge and stitch in place. Press.

LINING A GARMENT

*Garments are lined for a variety of
reasons – to make them more comfortable and
warmer in wear, to make sure they hang correctly or simply to
hide the inside! Whatever the reason, the lining
is made in the same way.*

There is one other great advantage to fully lining a garment – as all the raw edges are concealed, there is no need to neaten them! Lining a jacket or skirt also makes it easier to slip on and more hardwearing. In addition, with a light-coloured fabric, it stops the garment from being see-through. And in a fabric like linen it will help prevent creasing.

Fabrics designed especially to be used as a lining are widely available, but sometimes you cannot get the precise colour you need or they are not really the type of fabric you want. Basically, any light-weight fabric can be used as a lining. However, if the lining is there to help the garment hang correctly (such as the lining of a skirt), you should choose a slippery fabric so it will not cling.

Making and attaching the lining
Your pattern will give you details of exactly what sections are to be cut from the lining. These are usually the same pieces as are cut from the main fabric, but they often have some fabric trimmed from the hem edges or around the facing area. Half linings are sometimes used for skirts. Finishing just below hip level, at either the back or the front and back of the skirt, a half lining will help prevent 'seating' or bagginess in the skirt.

Again, your pattern will tell you how to join the lining pieces together – this is usually in exactly the same way as the outer sections, except that inter-facing is not used. Once the main sections are joined

and the whole lining shell is complete, the two are joined together. The lining will usually be attached both by seaming it in place and by hand stitching. If it is a skirt lining, the waist edge will be seamed in with the waistband, and if it is a jacket or coat, the lining will be seamed to the facing edges. Hand stitching is generally used to attach a skirt lining to the zip tape around the zip opening and to attach a jacket or coat lining to the hem edges. A lining is usually slightly longer than the garment, so that a little pleat forms in the lining, which helps the garment hang correctly.

It is a good idea to work a few backstitches (see page 15) through both the lining and the main section seam allowances at the underarm point to help hold the sleeve linings in place.

Shoulder pads
Many lined garments have shoulder pads inserted between the two layers of fabric, and it is best to attach these to the main fabric shell before closing the lining hem.

Position the shoulder pad so that the straight edge is level with the armhole seam allowance. Stitch it in place with a line of hand stitches worked through the armhole seam allowances and the shoulder pad, placing the stitching as close as you can to the seamline. You can attach the inner edge of the pad to the shoulder seam allowances – but there is no real need to, as the lining will help keep the pad flat.

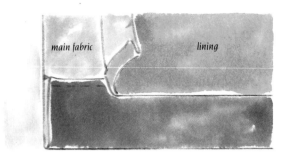

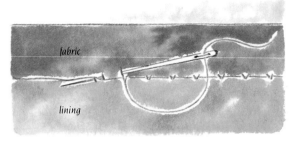

◆ Once you have seamed the lining in place, your pattern will usually tell you to press the seam allowances along the remaining raw edges to the wrong side. This pressed edge is then hand stitched to the inside of the outer section – usually through the hem allowance. The little pleat that forms in the lining helps the garment hang correctly because it prevents the lining from distorting the outer shell.

◆ **Slip-stitch** the lining in place using one strand of sewing thread. Start at the righthand edge of the 'seam' and secure the thread. Take a small stitch through the main fabric, taking great care that this goes through the hem allowance only and does not show on the right side, and then pick up one or two strands of the lining along the pressed edge. Continue along the edge in this way, fastening off at the end.

LOOSE LININGS

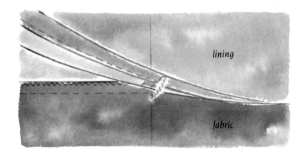

◆ A skirt lining, and sometimes a coat or dress lining, will be left loose at the hem edge, in which case it is a good idea to neaten the raw hem and seam allowance edges for about 20–30cm (8–12in) above the hem edge. If the lining hem edge is to be left loose, finish the edge with a narrow machined hem. To help keep the lining in place, you will need to make bar tacks at the side seam points to hold the lining without restraining its movement.

◆ To make a bar tack, attach double thread to the main fabric seamline at a point just below the neatened hem edge and make a chain of threads about 3cm (1¼in) long. Make the chain like a crochet chain by pulling loops of thread through the loop you start with. Once the chain is the length you need, thread the needle through the loop, to fasten the chain, and attach this end of the chain to the corresponding point on the inside of the lining hem edge.

TAILOR MADE

*With its clean, uncluttered lines, this fully
lined tailored jacket is not difficult to make yet is a versatile
addition to any wardrobe. The Chanel-style neckline
avoids the need for complicated lapels, and the
shoulder pads add important definition.*

YOU WILL NEED

1.70m (1⅞yd) of 150cm
(60in) wide fabric with or
without nap

1.30m (1½yd) of 150cm
(60in) wide lining fabric

80cm (⅞yd) of 90cm (36in)
wide iron-on interfacing

5 buttons

Pair of shoulder pads

Matching thread

YOU COULD USE

Any medium- to heavy-
weight fabric, such as the
wool/mohair tweed used
here, corduroy or coating. If
you use a fabric with a high
wool content, it will be
easier to press and you will
achieve a much neater
sleevehead.

SIZES

To fit size 10, 12–14 or 16

Finished length from back
neck 65cm (25½in)

MAKING PATTERN

Following Main Fabric Pattern
and Layout Diagram on page 70,
draw out pattern pieces full size –
one square represents 5cm (2in).
Hem allowance of 5cm (2in) and
seam allowances of 1.5cm (⅝in)
are included throughout. Transfer
all pattern markings onto pattern
pieces.

ADJUSTING THE SIZE

Pattern given is **for size 12–14**. To
adjust size, cut through Front and
Back pattern pieces along dotted
line. **For size 10,** overlap pieces by
1.5cm (⅝in). **For size 16,** insert a
strip of paper 1.5cm (⅝in) wide.
Re-draw shoulder and hem cutting lines.

CUTTING OUT

Fold fabrics in half lengthwise,
with right sides facing, and pin
pattern pieces to fabrics following
relevant Layout Diagram on page
70. Cut out all pieces and transfer
pattern markings onto fabric.
From main fabric: Front – cut 2;
Side Front: cut 2; Back – cut to
fold; Side Back – cut 2; Pocket –
cut 2; Back Neck Facing – cut to
fold; Top Sleeve – cut 2; Under
Sleeve – cut 2.
From lining fabric: Front – cut 2,
trimming off facing and hem section beyond broken line; Side
Front – cut 2, trimming 6cm
(2⅜in) from hem edge; Back – cut
to fold, trimming off neck section
above broken line and 6cm
(2⅜in) from hem edge; Side Back
– cut 2, trimming 6cm (2⅜in)
from hem edge; Pocket – cut 2,
trimming 7cm (2¾in) from shorter upper edge; Top Sleeve – cut 2,
trimming 6cm (2⅜in) from hem
edge; Under Sleeve – cut 2, trimming 6cm (2⅜in) from hem edge.
From interfacing: Front – cut 2,
cutting to marked fold line; Back
Neck Facing – cut one to fold.

MAKING UP

All seams are stitched with right
sides facing and pressed open
unless stated otherwise.
1 ◆ Apply interfacing to wrong
side of self-facings of Fronts, and
to Back Neck Facing.
2 ◆ Stitch Side Fronts to Fronts
along side front panel seams. In

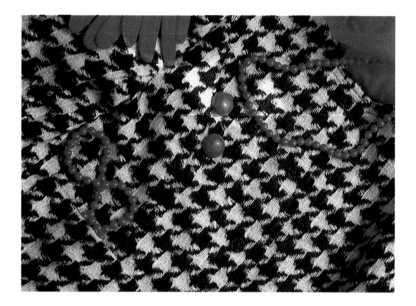

same way, stitch Side Backs to Back along side back panel seams, matching dots. Press seams.

3 ◆ Stitch Pocket Lining to Pocket along upper edge, leaving a 6cm (2¼in) opening. Press seam towards lining. Fold pocket in half with right sides facing, folding along fold line shown on pattern, and stitch along side and lower edges. Trim seam and corners. Turn pocket right side out and press. Hand stitch opening in pocket/lining seam closed. Topstitch opening edge of pocket, working first row of stitching 1.5cm (⅝in) from finished edge, and second row midway between first row and finished edge.

4 ◆ Place pockets onto right side of fronts, positioning lower edge of pocket 8cm (3in) above lower edge of front, and inner edge of pocket 9cm (3½in) away from opening edge fold line. Stitch

pocket in place close to edges. Press.

5 ◆ Stitch fronts to back along side seams and shoulder seams. Press. Stitch shoulder seams of front facings and Back Neck Facing. Press.

6 ◆ Fold front and back neck facings to right side along marked fold line and stitch facings to main sections along neck edge. Stitch across lower edge of front facings 5cm (2in) above lower edge. Trim and clip seam and turn facings to wrong side. Press.

7 ◆ Fold 5cm (2in) hem allowance to inside along remaining lower edge and stitch in place. Press.

8 ◆ Stitch Top Sleeves to Under Sleeves, along front and back sleeve seams. Press. Fold 5cm (2in) hem allowance to wrong side around cuff edge, and stitch in place. Press.

9 ◆ Matching dots, notches and sleevehead dots to shoulder

seams, insert sleeves into armholes (see page 41), easing in fullness over sleevehead section between dots. Press seam flat. Insert shoulder pads.

10 ◆ Make up Lining in same way as for main fabric, following steps 2,5,8 and 9. Press 1.5cm (⅝in) to wrong side along lower edge of body and sleeves.

11 ◆ Stitch front and back lining to main section along inner edge of front and back neck facings – start and stop stitching at dots above hem edge. Trim and clip seam and press towards lining. Turn jacket right side out, and push sleeve linings down inside sleeves.

12 ◆ Position folded lower edges of body and sleeve lining 3.5cm (1⅜in) above hem edges of main fabric and neatly slip-stitch in place; a small pleat will form at lower edge of lining for ease when wearing.

13 ◆ Finish stitching lining/front facing seam by hand, and slip-stitch inner edge of front facing to hem allowance below lining.

14 ◆ Topstitch front opening and neck edges. Work first row of stitching 1.5cm (⅝in) from finished edge, and second row midway between first row and finished edge. Press.

15 ◆ Make 5 horizontal buttonholes (see page 37) in right front. Position end of all buttonholes 2.5cm (1in) in from front opening edge, top buttonhole 2.5cm (1in) below neck seam and remaining buttonholes 11cm (4¼in) apart. Attach buttons to left front to correspond.

DECORATIVE DETAILS

A simple garment can be turned into
something quite stunning by the addition of a decorative trim –
but it must be attached in the right way.

Belts and ties

These fall into two groups – those that are stiff and hold their shape, and those that are soft and fluid. If a belt or tie is to be stiff, it will obviously need to have an interfacing. It is unlikely that the interfacing you are using for the main sections will be stiff enough, so choose another weight. Buckram, for example, is designed for this. It is also possible to buy belt-making kits from good haberdashery (notions) stores.

Braids, ribbons and lace

These can be attached by hand or by machine but it is best to start by basting them into the position you want them. Unless the trim is very narrow, it will need to be attached along both edges. If you are hand stitching it in place, attach it in the same way as you would a lining to a hem. If machine stitching it, you can either work a row of straight stitches just inside the trim edge or a narrow zigzag stitch over the trim edge. If the trim is very narrow – such as a Russia braid – simply stitch it in place straight down the middle. Rickrack is also best attached this way.

Lace trims can be attached in the same way as braid or ribbon. However, if you are making lingerie, nightwear or evening wear, they can be attached flat to finish an edge. The method of attaching lace trims which is shown opposite can also be used to attach lace motifs.

MAKING SOFT BELTS AND TIES

♦ Ties, and soft belts that will tie, are best made from two layers of fabric – a strip folded in half or two narrow strips – seamed together. Whichever way they are made, remember to leave an opening somewhere along one edge so that you can turn the belt or tie through to the right side.

♦ Narrow ties can be made from bias-cut strips. If these are not pressed flat, they will roll to form a narrow tube of fabric. If you want a 'fuller' tube, thread knitting yarn through to help the tube hold its shape. Knot the end, pulling it up tight to form a ball effect, and cut off the remaining end.

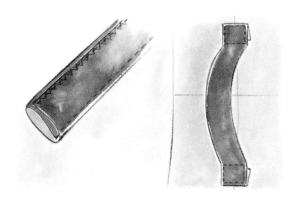

◆ Belt loops are best made in one long strip that is then cut into separate loops. Cut a strip of fabric three times the width of the final loop and, if not on the selvedge, neaten one long edge. Fold the strip lengthwise into thirds, with the neatened edge visible, and stitch close to both long edges. Press it flat and cut it into the required lengths. Then either catch them in the waistband seams, or turn each end under 6mm (¼in), press, and stitch in place.

◆ If a braid is to be bent so that it will go along a curved edge, make sure you buy a trim that is flexible; most ribbons are not. Start by basting it in place along both edges so that you can gently ease in the extra fullness along the inside of the curve. Press the braid once it has been basted and, if necessary, steam it to shrink in any remaining fullness. The final stitching can now be worked, the basting removed and the final press given.

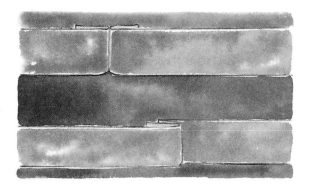

◆ If the ends of a trim do not disappear into a seam they must meet neatly. Depending on the bulk of the trim, the raw ends can either be folded under, so that the two folded ends butt up against each other, or one end can be turned under and this fold can overlap the other raw end, covering it completely.

◆ To attach lace trim, place it over the right side of the raw edge that it is to be attached to and baste it in place. Stitch using a medium-width zigzag stitch, following the outline of the lace. Using small, sharp scissors and working from the wrong side, trim away the remaining fabric seam allowances.

GOING INTO DETAIL

*Details can make all the difference to the
styling and professional finish of a garment, as in this classic
lined waistcoat with its mock welt pockets and
half-belt at the back.*

YOU WILL NEED

70cm (⅞yd) of 150cm (60in) wide fabric with or without nap

1.35m (1½yd) of 150cm (60in) wide lining fabric

70cm of 90cm (36in) wide iron-on interfacing

4 buttons

Matching thread

YOU COULD USE

Any medium- to heavy-weight fabric, such as the fancy tweed used here, velvet or brocade

SIZES

To fit size 10, 12–14 or 16

Finished length from back neck 59cm (23¼in)

MAKING PATTERN

Following Pattern and Lining Layout Diagram on page 70, draw out pattern pieces full size – one square represents 5cm (2in). (You need to make only one Back pattern piece as they are both the same.) Seam allowances of 1.5cm (⅝in) are included throughout. Transfer all pattern markings onto pattern pieces.

ADJUSTING THE SIZE

Pattern given is for size 12–14. To adjust size, cut through Front and Back pattern pieces along dotted line. For size 10, overlap pieces by 1.5cm (⅝in). For size 16, insert a strip of paper 1.5cm (⅝in) wide. Re-draw shoulder and hem cutting lines.

CUTTING OUT

Fold lining fabric in half length-wise, with right sides facing, and pin pattern pieces to fabrics following Pattern and Lining Layout Diagram. Cut out all pieces and transfer pattern markings onto fabric.

From lining fabric: Front – cut 2; Back – cut 2 to fold; Tie – cut 2.
From main fabric: Front – cut 2; Pocket Welt pieces 14cm (5½in) wide by 9cm (3½in) deep – cut 2.
From interfacing: Front – cut 2.

MAKING UP

All seams are stitched with right sides facing then are pressed open unless stated otherwise.

1 ◆ Fold Pocket Welt in half lengthwise with right sides facing, and stitch across ends. Trim seam and corners and turn Welts right side out. Press. Topstitch close to and 6mm (¼in) from long pressed edge. Neaten long raw edges together.

2 ◆ Apply interfacing to wrong side of Fronts. Lay Pocket Welt onto right side of Front with raw edges against marked placement line and folded edge towards hem edge of Front. Stitch Welt in place by stitching 1.5cm (⅝in) below raw edges through all layers. Press Welt upwards, to cover neatened edges, and stitch ends in place by topstitching through all layers close to ends of Welt. Repeat for other Welt.

3 ◆ Fold each Tie in half lengthwise with right sides together and stitch along length and across unnotched end. Trim seam and corners and turn Tie right side out. Press, placing seam along pressed edge. Topstitch Tie close to and 6mm (¼in) from both long edges and from seamed short edge. Press.

4 ◆ Lay a Tie onto right side of each Front, matching notches, and baste open end of Tie in place. Stitch Fronts to one Back piece along side seams, enclosing Ties in seams, and press. This completes outer shell.

5 ◆ Stitch Front Linings to remaining Back piece along side seam edges. Press. Press seam allowances to wrong side across shoulder seam edges of this inner shell.

6 ◆ With right sides facing, matching shoulder seamlines and side seams and notches, stitch lining shell to outer shell in four stages. First, stitch shells together along entire front neck and opening edges, and front and back hem edges, pivoting stitching at corners. Second, stitch back shells together along back neck edge. And finally, stitch shells together along both armhole edges.

7 ◆ Trim corners and seam allowances, and snip into seam allowance along curves. Turn waistcoat right side out through one open shoulder edge and press, placing seams along pressed edges.

8 ◆ Stitch Fronts to outer Back section across shoulder seams, keeping inner shell sections free, and press. Now slip-stitch pressed inner shell shoulder seams closed. Press. Topstitch close to and 6mm (¼in) from entire neck, front opening, hem and armhole edges. Press.

9 ◆ Make 4 horizontal buttonholes in right front. Position ends of buttonholes 1.5cm (⅝in) in from front opening edge, top buttonhole 1.5cm (⅝in) below corner where front neck slope begins, lowest buttonhole 4cm (1½in) above corner at lower edge of front opening edge and remaining 2 buttonholes evenly spaced between. Attach buttons to left front to correspond.

Pattern and Layout Diagrams

On these pages are Pattern Diagrams for drawing
up all the patterns used in the book, and Layout Diagrams
for positioning your pattern pieces on the fabric. For many
patterns the two types of diagram are combined.

◆ Enlarge the patterns to the correct size on
a photocopier; or draw up your own grid,
making each square 5cm (2in), then copy
the shapes onto the grid, square by square.

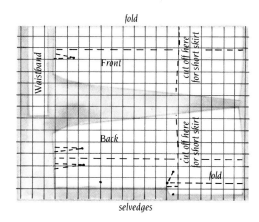

◆ Pattern and Layout Diagram for skirts on pages 38-9

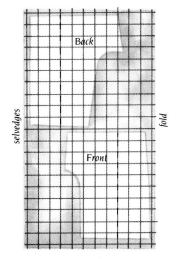

◆ Pattern and Layout Diagram
for shorts on pages 20-1

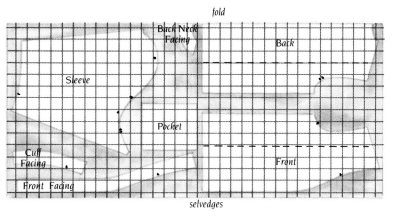

◆ Pattern and Layout Diagram for jacket on pages 28-9

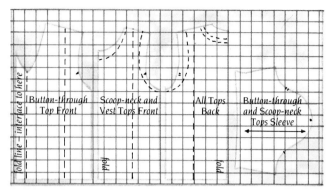

◆ Pattern Diagram for tops on pages 32-4

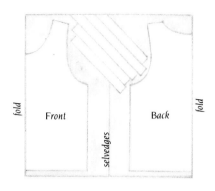

◆ Layout Diagram for vest top on pages 32-4

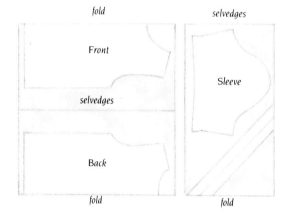

◆ Layout Diagram for scoop-neck top on pages 32-4

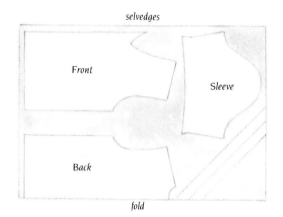

◆ Layout Diagram for button-through top on pages 32-4

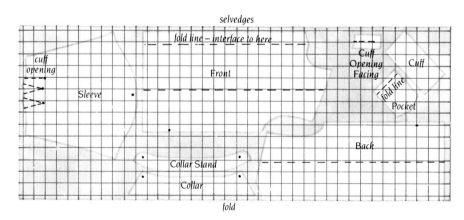

◆ Pattern and Layout Diagram for overshirt on pages 43-4

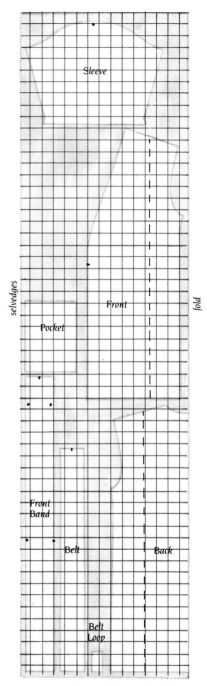

◆ Pattern and Layout Diagram for kimono on pages 30-1

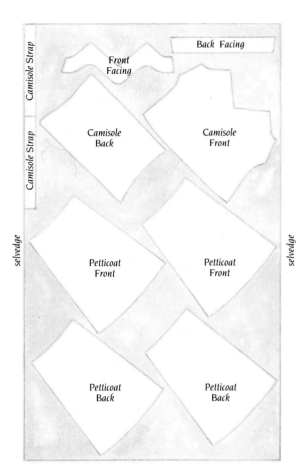

◆ Layout Diagram for camisole and petticoat on pages 54-6

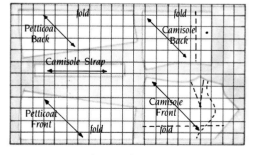

◆ Pattern Diagram for camisole and petticoat on pages 54-6

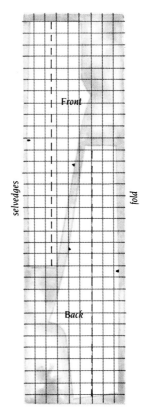

◆ Pattern and Layout
Diagram for leggings
on pages 50-1

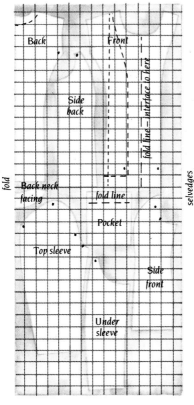

◆ Main Fabric Pattern and Layout
Diagram for jacket on pages 59-61

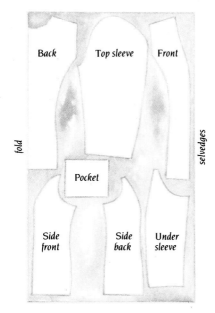

◆ Lining Layout Diagram for jacket
on pages 59-61

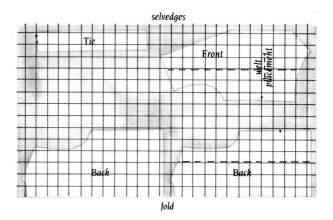

◆ Pattern and Lining Layout Diagram for waistcoat on pages 64-5

INDEX

ACKNOWLEDGEMENTS

The publishers would like to thank Country Pine and Collectables, Sidmouth Street, Devizes, Wiltshire, for kindly allowing photography on their premises.